DISCOVER
JESUS

Mark Finley
with David B. Smith

Pacific Press Publishing Association
Boise, Idaho
Oshawa, Ontario, Canada

Edited by Russell Holt
Designed by Tim Larson
Cover art by Harry Anderson
Typeset in 10/12 Janson

Library of Congress Cataloging-in-Publication Data:

ISBN 0-8163-1149-8

93 94 95 96 97 • 5 4 3 2 1

Contents

Introduction 5

Chapter 1 The Conspiracy Exposed
           The Resurrected Jesus 7

Chapter 2 Messenger From Beyond the Stars
           Jesus the Revealer 19

Chapter 3 The Blood Tells Its Story
           Jesus the Sacrificed Lamb. 31

Chapter 4 A King in the Barn
           Jesus Our Example 45

Chapter 5 Showdown at Sundown
           Jesus, Lord of the Sabbath 59

Chapter 6 The Judge Who Faces Sentencing
           Jesus Our Intercessor 73

Chapter 7 The Great War Is Over
           Jesus the Triumphant King 85

Introduction

Evening came to Tiberias as sunset illuminated the sky with crimson glory. Sunset faded into a clear night, with stars reflecting like diamonds off the lake. A full moon cast its pale glow across the peaceful waters of the Sea of Galilee.

I sat quietly on the water's edge, reflecting about the Christ who had taught on Galilee's shores, walked on Galilee's waters, and calmed Galilee's deadly whitecapped waves. My mind drifted back over the centuries, and I imagined meeting Jesus right here in His land. There are so many things I'd like to ask Him, so many things I would like to share. No one knows me so well, yet loves me so much as He. No one else knows all my weaknesses, understands all my needs, and is capable of providing me with so much help.

In the stillness of that Galilean night, I found myself in another age, longing to meet this Christ face to face, longing to discover Jesus afresh, longing to get to know Him better.

Maybe you've had a desire to meet Him too. Or, if you've already met Him, perhaps you want to know Him better. I'd like to invite you on a journey to the Holy Land with me to discover Jesus anew.

Why not accompany our film crew on this thrilling journey that follows the footsteps of Jesus? In these pages, we'll visit Bethlehem, the city of His birth; Nazareth, His boyhood home; Jerusalem, the city that rejected Him. Then Gethsemane, Calvary, the Garden Tomb, and Ascension Mountain.

Reliving the experiences of this unique Man's life, we will surely get to know Him better. And by knowing Him better, we will love Him more. His forgiveness, His acceptance, His life-changing power are just as available today as they were two thousand years ago. His offer of new life is just as real.

Again, I am indebted to my able research assistant and writing colleague, David B. Smith, for his invaluable contribution to this volume. Martin Weber, associate editor of *Ministry* magazine, in his unique and creative style, also provided us with invaluable inspirational insight. Together, we earnestly pray that you will genuinely meet the open-armed Saviour of Galilee just as truly as if you had been sitting by this lake two thousand years ago and met Him face to face. May these pages lead you to *Discover Jesus*.

Mark A. Finley

1

The Conspiracy Exposed

The Resurrected Jesus

Chapter 1

The Conspiracy Exposed

It was a meeting of desperate minds. High-level political leaders in a rendezvous at midnight with the power elite of the corrupt religious establishment. In hushed tones they whispered urgently among themselves about the events of the weekend.

The planned murder had gone according to design. The enemy they had marked for death . . . was dead. Victory seemed assured. Their sinister grab for power, their undercover conspiracy, had succeeded beyond their dreams.

There was just one final concern. Only one thing spelled the difference between lasting success and crushing defeat. The enemy they had killed must stay dead. Tomorrow, next year, for the next thousand years—everything hinged on there being a body in that tomb!

* * *

The book you are holding contains the story of one of my most rewarding spiritual adventures. For nearly three weeks in September 1992, the "It Is Written" production staff and I traveled to the very sites where the conspiracy I just described took place. We journeyed to the fascinating land of Israel for what turned out to be one of the most intriguing journeys of a lifetime.

I'm so grateful that you've joined me for the trip! The seven television productions we filmed in Israel become in these pages seven thought-provoking studies you and I can explore together.

The title of this book gives away what we're here to do together: *Discover Jesus.* Israel is the homeland of a certain Man—a very real, flesh-and-blood Man—whose name was Jesus. This Man Jesus walked through the very areas we're about to explore. He climbed the hills around the ancient city of Jerusalem. He and His followers drank from the streams that trickle through the terrain of this land of Israel.

But what do we want to discover about this Jesus? Certain fundamental questions must be answered if our faith is to be intelligent. Why did this person Jesus come here? What were His purposes, His goals? What's on His résumé? What did He accomplish—or fail to accomplish? How did He live? What was He like?

And then—what was the end of His experience? What does the last chapter reveal? As the final credits roll, when we get to the last page, what do we discover about this one Man—Jesus, citizen of Jerusalem—whose name is known by nearly every inhabitant on earth two thousand years later?

Come with me to one of Jerusalem's most frequently visited tourist sites: the Garden Tomb. Right away, I'm sure a perplexing question has popped into your mind. You're probably thinking: "Pastor Finley, shouldn't you start in Bethlehem, where Jesus was born? Isn't it rather odd to start with His death rather than His birth?"

That's a good question. But the answer is "Not really." Let me tell you why.

Remember the conspiracy I just described to you—everything hinged on there being a body in that tomb. The group of conspirators had plotted to kill their enemy, this Man Jesus. They *had* killed Him. He was dead and buried—for good, they hoped.

But today millions of men and women around this globe believe that tomb is empty. People everywhere for two thousand years have staked everything they love, everything they believe in and stand for, on that one great, daring headline: **JESUS RISEN FROM THE DEAD!**

The idea of the resurrection of Jesus Christ is the dramatic, pivotal pillar of all Christianity. For millions of people, all other truth rests on *that* truth. The entire kingdom of God stands or falls on this idea of an empty tomb here in the city of Jerusalem.

The same was true for those conspirators—and for the force of evil that drove them on. If the tomb had a body in it, victory was theirs. The kingdom of darkness would triumph. But if that Jerusalem gravesite was empty on Sunday morning, their carefully crafted power base would come crashing down with an echo that would not die for millenniums to come.

There's an expression that Christian ministers often like to use: "The Great Controversy." It refers to the far-flung, universal conflict between good and evil, between God and His enemy Lucifer, or Satan. And that whole war climaxes over this question of an empty tomb. If it's empty, God wins. If not, then . . .

Well, then what? During this *Discover Jesus* adventure, we'll find out together just what really was at stake.

In any case, we stand at the door to the tomb. You can see now why we came here first. We start with the Garden Tomb because if the tomb is not empty, then there's no point going on. If the resurrection story is itself a hoax, a conspiracy of some kind, then a book entitled *Discover Jesus* is nothing but an empty, tragic joke.

The great apostle Paul sensed that the whole of Christianity hinged on the resurrection. In fact, in writing to the men and women of Corinth, he admitted it right out. Listen to this:

> If Christ is not risen, then our preaching is vain and your faith is also vain. Yes, and we are found false witnesses of God, because we have testified of God that He raised up Christ. . . . And if Christ is not risen, your faith is futile; you are still in your sins! (1 Corinthians 15:14-17, NKJV).

Paul puts it right there on the line, don't you agree? "If that tomb isn't empty," he says, "then I'm a liar, Christianity itself is a lie, and all our hopes are as dead as the rocks in these hills of Israel." Everything rests on the answer to this question: Did Jesus come out of that tomb?

Think about it. Only Christ the Son of God—in fact, only Christ who was God Himself—could come out of that tomb. The question of Jesus being divine hinges on the resurrection.

The truth of the Bible itself is at stake. If the biggest story in God's Word is a lie, who cares what the rest of it says?

And bringing it right down close to home, if Christ didn't come out of that tomb—then neither will anybody else. If Jesus is still dead and buried today, then every funeral you ever attend is the end, with no hope of tomorrow. Paul himself admits that, in verses 17 and 18 of 1 Corinthians 15. "If Christ is not risen, . . . then also those who have fallen asleep in Christ have perished" (NKJV).

So much rides on what we decide about this one Man's grave!

Well, we look together into this tomb—and it's empty. It's easy to visualize the body of this Man, Jesus, resting on that small ledge through Friday night, through the Sabbath hours, and then early into Sunday morning. But what happened next?

A sign outside the Garden Tomb contains eight words from Luke 24:6. "He is not here, for He is risen!" I personally feel this is the greatest announcement ever made. *If* it's true. Let me say it again: *If* it's true, these are the most earthshaking eight words the universe has ever witnessed. *If* those eight words are true.

Now, friend, let me open my heart to you. I'm a Christian minister. I've been a worker in the Christian faith for some twenty-five years now. So you'll understand when I tell you that I've staked my entire career and my life and my family's future on the validity of those eight words. I believe them with all my heart, and I've given every facet of my existence to the cause of Christianity based on that belief.

But how about you? You've probably heard since you were a child that there was a person named Jesus who rose from the dead. Maybe you've believed it, maybe not. Maybe you haven't paid much attention. But now, here we are facing this question—this suggestion of a conspiracy. Whom do we believe? If our entire belief system boils down to this one question, then we need to study it carefully and answer it carefully, don't you think?

As you are reading these words, you may be saying right now: "Mr. Finley, I'm not going to believe some story about a man rising from the dead just because *you* say so. I don't even know you!"

And do you know what I'd say to that? "Good for you!"

This is too important a question for you to let some TV preacher come along and fool you. This question—above all questions—deserves your own careful study, your own thoughtful consideration.

Think harder about this than you've ever thought about anything else in your life: Is this fundamental claim of Christianity valid? Who is really telling the truth?

The fact that this tomb is empty today doesn't solve our question, does it? Life is never that easy. Several questions come to mind right away:

Is this even the correct place? No one knows for sure. Several locations in Jerusalem are suggested. Tourists visit each of them. But none of these tombs has a body resting in it.

Of course, as we think and study this great question carefully, we remember something important. Early that very Sunday morning, the tomb *was* empty. There's no question about that. Both sides in the conflict that Sunday morning admitted—with very different emotions, I'm sure—that the tomb which once held the body of Jesus, executed prisoner from Nazareth, now had nobody in it.

One group, the followers of Jesus, began to tell the story of the resurrection—and they've been doing it ever since. The other side, the original conspirators, had a story to tell as well. Out of that turmoil-filled Sunday morning came a story of counterconspiracy. A double twist in this great controversy in which the killers turned the tables on their enemies and started a propaganda campaign of their own.

You can read their story in the book of Matthew. Whether or not it's a believable cover story has been debated right down to today. You be the judge. Their version? "His disciples came at night and stole Him away while we slept" (Matthew 28:13, NKJV).

Of course, if you read the whole verse and the one before it, you find how the conspirators prepared these instructions: "*Tell them*, 'His disciples came at night and stole Him away' " (emphasis supplied). And if you read the verse after, you discover bribe money changing hands. Fascinating drama, rivaling any political scandals our twentieth-century leaders have come up with.

So who's telling the truth? Are the bones of this Man named Jesus still decomposing in some secret hiding place in Israel? That's a disturbing thought to any Christian believer, yet any thinking man or woman wants to look at all the evidence. Is the entire Christian faith built upon a desperate lie concocted during a weekend of tragedy and then perpetuated ever since by eleven brave but brokenhearted disciples and their followers? Something to think about, isn't it?

Let's shift scenery for just a moment as I share a story with you. It's the story of a man, perhaps much like yourself, who had a fierce debate with himself about this question of a resurrected Jesus Christ.

Chuck Colson. Many Democrats still can't help clenching their fists a little bit when they hear the name. Chuck, you see, was one of the top political operatives working for President Richard Nixon during the Watergate scandal from 1972 through 1974. His skill with dirty tricks and political shenanigans helped give the GOP a big win over George McGovern in the 1972 election.

I wish I had several hours to tell you Chuck Colson's amazing conversion story. If you have the opportunity, read his wonderful book *Born Again*. It's a moving, dramatic experience of how some of his bitterest political enemies reached out to him during a time of great legal turmoil and led him to accept Jesus as his Saviour.

Today Chuck leads a ministry called Prison Fellowship. He's a wonderfully thought-provoking author and shares unique insights that came out of his own prison experiences following the Watergate trials nearly twenty years ago.

Chuck was not the kind of man to accept the idea of Christianity just because his friends suggested it. He had a fine legal mind, and he set out to explore with cold, pencil-sharpened logic the claims of Christianity. As he did so, he realized with a chill that his own experience in Watergate was itself the most compelling proof that the resurrection story was absolute truth.

Watergate, you remember, was itself a conspiracy—a few powerful men caught up in a crime that they had to cover up. A break-in followed by obstruction of justice, hush money, illegal conversations, diverting the FBI's search for truth. All of it had to be kept under wraps. A blanket lie had to protect them all.

Things went well, Chuck remembers—for about two weeks. All at once things began to unravel. Despite the fact that only a few powerful men knew the awful truth, the whole fabric of their coverup began to break apart at the seams.

Do you know what caused everything to fall apart? I'm sure you can imagine. The threat of punishment, of jail time. As soon as prosecutors began to hint about prison terms, one by one, those Watergate conspirators began to look to get out. To plea-bargain. To cut a deal for themselves by singing a confession opera about the others.

Within months, the entire mess had leaked out, leaving the whole ugly story exposed. Almost everyone went to jail anyway; the president of the United States had to resign in disgrace. One simple lie could not be maintained.

And as Chuck Colson later searched—painstakingly—through these claims of Christianity, he realized that Watergate held the key to the truth about the resurrection of Jesus.

Now, let me unbalance the scales just a little bit. Watergate was about a few men protecting what they felt was a noble concept: democracy. Yes, mistakes had been made. But in their hearts, they felt that they were engaged in a coverup that, in the long run, would protect liberty and democracy and the United States Constitution and all the rest. In other words, they were committing a crime for a good cause. Or so they thought.

Remember, too, these were men at the very pinnacles of power. Unimagined luxuries were theirs at a snap of the fingers. Limos. Secret Service men. Helicopter trips to Camp David and food and drink provided by red-coated stewards standing on alert twenty-four hours a day. These men had something worth protecting.

And one thing more, as Colson points out. None of the Watergate men were threatened with execution or even long prison sentences. Most of them served very little time—less than a year in most cases. Yet, this small group of conspirators could not keep a lie together, even what they felt was a noble lie, for two weeks! Under the threat of country-club jail sentences, they cracked! Every one of them.

As Chuck, in his spiritual search, looked back, he suddenly realized a very down-to-earth truth. Conspiracies don't last! Even the good ones!

He considered the possibility that those eleven disciples *had* stolen the body of Jesus, buried Him in some lonely spot, and then, after drying their tears, begun to proclaim a resurrection story.

How many of them, Chuck wondered, would continue to preach a shameful lie under threat of death? How many believers would spend the rest of their lives and livelihoods to spread a story built on failure and falsehood, even to the point of turning down a stool pigeon's pot of gold? Even to the point of facing the lions or their own crucifixion crosses?

Paul Little, author of a book entitled *Know Why You Believe*, has this to say: "Men will die for what they *believe* to be true, though it may actually be false. They do not, however, die for what they *know* to be a lie." And Chuck Colson, of all men, could see that so clearly now. So it was with a renewed faith in this vital claim of Christianity that Colson became one of Jesus Christ's most ardent followers.

Now let me whisk you several thousand miles from Jerusalem to the streets of downtown Moscow in the former Soviet Union for a breathtaking climax to the first chapter in our journey.

It was in the Kremlin Congress Hall where for so many decades the Communist Party ruled the vast empire of the Soviet Union. But in March 1992—by the power of God—fellow believers and I presented a Christian evangelistic crusade here! What thrilling proof that the message of Christianity really does spring from the power of a risen Lord!

Two years earlier, in the summer of 1990, I had been in Russia for another series of meetings. I found the people there incredibly hungry for spiritual food. The news media gave us far more publicity than I had expected, with plenty of live TV coverage. One day, just before my meeting, a reporter came up to me and requested an interview. "I want to talk about Lenin," he said. "Tell me, is Lenin in heaven or in hell? I'd like a straight answer." He was a very earnest man.

Well, what do you say to such a question? I mentioned the dead leader's tomb and said, "Lenin is sleeping inside his mausoleum."

"Was he a good leader or a bad one?"

"All nations have their leaders," I told him. "Churchill, Lincoln, Mohammed, Lenin—all of them were able to influence millions. But they couldn't save anybody from damnation."

The reporter brushed aside my response and persisted in his original question. "Tell me, once and for all, what will be Lenin's ultimate fate?" (I think this reporter must have been the Soviet version of Sam Donaldson!)

I looked into his honest face, and I told him: "I believe history will condemn Lenin as one who oppressed his own people. As for his eternal fate, only God can pass judgment on that."

With that I launched into a Bible study on death and eternal life through Jesus. The reporter took careful notes, then thanked me and left. I didn't think much more about our conversation until a week later. The *Moscow Echo*, with a half million circulation at that time, ran a front-page feature entitled: "Where is Lenin now?" And then underneath it: "Only Mark Finley knows."

Inside, on page eight, was the complete Bible study I'd given him on the topic of death and the resurrection. In my meetings when I presented that same subject, I wish you could have seen the Russian audience respond to the good news of their risen Lord. They stood up and applauded when I told them, "Christ is risen!" What a moment that was for me!

You know, the Communist system tried and failed to stamp out faith in the risen Christ. Back around 1930, the Communist leader Bukharin traveled from Moscow to Kiev, where he addressed a large crowd on the subject of atheism. For one solid hour he viciously attacked Christianity with every weapon he could muster, seasoning logic with ridicule. Finally, after he thought he'd worn out everybody and destroyed any credibility left to Christianity, he confidently demanded: "Are there any questions out there?"

One man rose and came forward. He mounted the platform and stood beside the Communist leader. After looking back and forth across the audience, he shouted the ancient Orthodox greeting: "Christ has risen!" The vast assembly rose together and responded like a massive choir, "He is risen indeed!"

I've spent years working in these countries where European Communism has strangled itself on the rope of its own atheism. I wish you could see how the truth about the resurrection of Jesus has lighted a blazing fire through these lands. More believers than ever before are now worshiping Jesus as the resurrected Lord. You can ask people in the Kremlin Congress Hall or out on the streets, and they'll tell you: "Jesus came to this earth and died for our sins—and now His tomb is empty!" That empty tomb is filling hearts with hope here in the former Soviet Union and all around the world.

As you continue reading in order to discover Jesus for yourself, let me say it again: Without the resurrection there would be no hope. But *with* the resurrection, *with* the confidence of that wonderful doctrine ringing in our hearts, we have all the hope in the world! Jesus' own disciple, Peter, so crushed by the crucifixion of his Master, and then so thrilled by the resurrection, joined Paul in preaching about hope in 1 Peter 1:3. "In his great mercy he [God] has given us new birth into a living hope through the resurrection of Jesus Christ from the dead" (NIV).

Maybe this Man, Jesus, is a brand new figure to you. These might be the very first words you've read about Him. I hope that on all the pages to follow, you'll discover Jesus to be a Friend, as well as a resurrected Saviour.

Maybe you've been a follower of Christ for many years. You're in church every weekend; you've given your life to Him. And yet you're eager to know Him better—to have an even more fulfilling friendship with Him. Keep turning the pages! I think the things we'll explore together will help you draw even closer to Him.

Before we began taping these programs for television, one of my associates said, "Mark, really, there's not a person anywhere who doesn't need to discover Jesus." And that's so true. No matter what your background, no matter what your religious heritage, you and I both will be so blessed as we discover and *re*discover this Man, Jesus Christ of Jerusalem, who on a Sunday morning two thousand years ago, came out of the tomb in victory!

I'd like you today, wherever you are, to simply say, "Yes. Yes, Pastor Finley, I'm willing to consider the possibility that Jesus Christ is alive today. I'm willing to explore the evidence. I'm willing to think about the possibility that today I could have a new, exciting, life-changing friendship with a Man who lived twenty centuries ago because I believe He still is living today."

Won't you join me in saying "Yes" right now as you add your prayer to mine?

* * *

"Father in Heaven, today the world listens to two stories. One story is a conspiracy of death and defeat; the other is a promise of resurrection and an empty tomb. Today thoughtful men and women everywhere are considering the claims of a risen Christ. And I pray that You will make Yourself and Your Son Jesus very real to every reader right now. Thank You for the thrilling hope we can have when we sense the glorious truth that Jesus is alive as promised in Your Word, the Bible. Thank You, Jesus, and we pray it in Your risen name, Amen."

2

Messenger From Beyond the Stars

Jesus the Revealer

Chapter 2

Messenger From Beyond the Stars

Nothing can look so peaceful as the city of Jerusalem at night. It's quiet here in the Old City, not much changed from thousands of years ago.

But the silent blanket of night covers a powder keg of violence that has rocked this city for centuries. Jerusalem is in the crosshairs of military focus, the center of the eye of the storm. Holy wars, political wars, rabid tribal conflicts all seem to have a focus in this tiny bloodstained spot on the map.

From the 1990s right back through history to the early days of Jerusalem, messengers of peace placed their lives in jeopardy if they traveled to this city. One in particular set out to come here knowing before He started that His own death was guaranteed. Before the journey even began, He'd been warned—and yet He came anyway. Together let's find out why. Come with me to Bethlehem.

* * *

It's quite an experience to travel to the city of Bethlehem. I can remember as a boy hearing about the town where the Baby Jesus was born. To walk its streets and enter its churches and temples is a vivid reminder to me that these great old Bible stories are real! These things really did happen. Bethlehem still speaks to our hearts after all these centuries.

And it was in Bethlehem where a young girl named Mary had a baby boy. You know the story as well as any preacher can tell it, how Jesus was born in a manger—a feeding trough. Born in a stable because there wasn't any room in the inn.

It's a wonderful story. And every year it finds its way onto our Christmas cards and into the carols we sing. "Away in a Manger." "O Little Town of Bethlehem." "Silent Night."

But did you ever stop to ask yourself, Why?

There's a "why" to this strange and wonderful story we celebrate each year. What's different about this particular baby's birth? Why did the angels sing? What about this "virgin birth" anyway?

Most thought-provoking of all: Why was this Baby born? Did this one Baby, who grew up to be the Boy Jesus and then became the Man Jesus Christ, really come to this earth from a pre-existent life with God in heaven? And if He did, why? As we continue our fact-finding tour in this land of Israel, that's the answer we're looking for.

Now let's travel in our imagination to the old Jerusalem temple, where for centuries the Jewish people offered their daily sacrifices. Just think of the hundreds and thousands of lambs that were killed as offerings to God from this very spot. As the years went by, it was quite a river of blood that flowed from the heart of Jerusalem.

Hold that picture in your mind for a moment as I ask you a simple question:

"What is your picture of God?"

What do you think He is like? I wish I could send out a questionnaire to everyone who is reading these pages. If I could find the time, I'd love to read every answer and find out what kind of picture of God people have today. The children of Israel had a picture of God. And as we approach this old temple site in Jerusalem, we can't help but shake our heads as we think of what might have been in their minds.

Consider this: It had been more than four thousand years since God Himself had come down to the Garden of Eden and enjoyed face-to-face fellowship with Adam and Eve. Four thousand years of separation and sin had gone by. Four thousand years while the enemy of mankind had whispered lies about God into the ears of anyone who would listen.

You know, it takes an amazingly short time for public opinion to completely turn around. We can see that in our American political campaigns! In just a few generations—the time from Adam down to Noah—the human race had already declared itself to be an enemy to God. Just a few pages into your Bible, barely into the first few chapters of the book of Genesis, you can read what had already happened:

The Lord saw how great man's wickedness on the earth had become, and that every inclination of the thoughts of his heart was only evil all the time. The Lord was grieved that he had made man on the earth, and his heart was filled with pain (Genesis 6:5, 6, NIV).

Six chapters into Earth's history and God was already seen as the enemy. Think about this: God provided a way of escape from this planet's destruction, and only eight people trusted Him enough to take Him up on it and step aboard Noah's ark. After the Flood, of course, Satan worked upon the minds of thousands to portray God as the Vengeful Destroyer. And so it went.

Through it all, during the entire history of the Old Testament, we find God reaching out to His people. Protecting. Providing. Sending prophets to warn and draw Israel back to Him. Allowing trials and captivity for the sole purpose of waking up His slumbering children before their destruction was complete.

But by the time the Bethlehem story was about to take place, the enemy's public-relations campaign was nearly complete. The children of Israel were suffocating under the iron rule of secular, pagan Rome. Centuries of bondage had extinguished their faith in God.

And religion? The Jewish nation was caught up in a thicket of religious confusion. Their detailed system of sacrifices had become a sterile ritual that had long before lost its meaning. Most people saw only the blood of the animals and the clinking coins of the money-changers as they bought and sold an empty form of salvation.

Really, is it much different today? You know, many of the same perceptions that had captivated the consciences of people twenty centuries ago still linger. "God is a destroying deity." "God is a vengeful tyrant, extinguishing the lives of those who displease Him." "God doesn't love—He only governs." Maybe even in the 1990s we might get a few questionnaires back with those statements marked "Yes."

Jesus grew up in the town of Nazareth in just such an environment of confusion. He lived among a people whose picture of their God had been clouded almost beyond recognition. And then—He began His ministry among them.

Right away, things began to happen. You see, not only did Jesus perform all the miracles you and I have heard so much about, but He also began to say some things about Himself. He made three claims about Himself, and those three claims reveal so much about this Messenger who came from beyond the stars.

The first thing Jesus said was that He was God. Time and time again, He stated that headline-making claim: "I am the Son of God."

Others said it too. The thief on the cross. The Roman centurion who watched Jesus die. His followers. One of Jesus' closest disciples, John, stated this truth in a most interesting way. You can read it in his book. "In the beginning was the Word, and the Word was with God, and the Word was God. . . . And the Word was made flesh, and dwelt among us" (John 1:1, 14, KJV).

A little later, we'll consider in greater detail this bold and thrilling idea that the Man Jesus was actually God. But let's look at His second and third claims as well.

Second, Jesus also claimed that the Father had sent Him. Jesus wasn't just any random baby who happened to be born in a stable. God sent Him! Probably the most-quoted words in the world are these: "For God so loved the world, that he *gave* His only begotten Son, that whosoever believeth in him should not perish, but have everlasting life" (John 3:16, KJV, emphasis supplied).

"Before Abraham was, I am" (John 8:58, KJV), Jesus once said to the priests. Here we find that Jesus existed with God before coming to earth and that He was sent as a gift from God. Oh, friend, never forget it—Jesus is God's gift! He didn't come here on His own!

Jesus' third claim is the greatest of all. He said that He and His Father were just like each other.

Picture Jesus sitting around a supper table with those twelve roughly dressed disciples as He teaches them about God's kingdom. All of a sudden, these six words come out of His lips: "I and my Father are one" (John 10:30, KJV).

Or maybe we can listen in during the Bible study during which the disciples are wondering out loud what God the Father is like—just as we sometimes do. Jesus, in His own patient way, tells them, "If you really knew me, you would know my Father as well. From now on, you do know him and have seen him" (John 14:7, NIV).

Philip leans forward and says, "Jesus, show us the Father, and that'll be enough for us" (see verse 8).

And Jesus, still so patient as His disciples learn, replies:

"Don't you know me, Philip, even after I have been among you such a long time? Anyone who has seen me has seen the Father. . . . The words I say to you are not just my own. Rather, it is the Father, living in me, who is doing his work. Believe me when I say that I am in the Father and the Father is in me" (verses 9-11, NIV).

Wonderful words—*if* we can believe them.

"Jesus is God."

"Jesus was sent by God."

"Jesus is just like God."

A pastor friend of mine once had a Bible student say to him, "I kind of like Jesus, but I don't like God."

"How come?"

"Because Jesus is meek and mild, but God is stern and full of wrath."

Have you ever harbored similar thoughts? Listen to these five wonderful words spoken so earnestly by Jesus: "The Father himself loves you" (John 16:27, NIV).

One of my very favorite volumes on the life of Jesus, *The Desire of Ages*, contains this memorable gem: "The gift of Christ reveals the Father's heart. It testifies that the thoughts of God toward us are 'thoughts of peace, and not of evil.' Jer. 29:11" (page 57).

Yes, the thoughts of Jesus toward us and the thoughts of God toward us are one and the same! If we can believe these three claims Jesus made, it's the best news anyone can ever hear. Can we believe what Jesus said about Himself and His Father?

In the first chapter of this book I encouraged you to study for yourself the claims of this Man named Jesus. Don't take the word of others. You need to discover for yourself whether these three bold statements can hold the foundation of your faith.

Let me ask you a question of logic: What can you say about anyone who says he is God? Obviously, anybody can *say* such a thing; the question is, How can we decide whether he's telling the truth?

In my public speaking and travels, I've heard many people say: "I believe Jesus was a great teacher. He had some insights that the entire world ought to pay attention to. I think of Jesus in the same light as Buddha or Confucius or Plato or Aristotle or some of the other great thinkers."

Have you ever heard people take that point of view? "Oh, I like the Sermon on the Mount," they say. "Love your neighbor—the Golden Rule. That's good; we ought to follow it. But Jesus being God? I just don't see that." Thomas Jefferson was one who saw Jesus this way—as a great world teacher, but not as God. In fact, he went through his own Bible, marking through references to Jesus as God.

Well, let me tell you something. The great Christian writer C. S. Lewis came up with the all-time, number-one argument destroying that train of thought. If you've never read his book *Mere Christianity*, I urge you to get a copy. Lewis argues it is utter nonsense to say that Jesus was a great teacher and at the same time deny that He is God.

Here in a nutshell is what Lewis says: When a man claims to be God (as Jesus did), you can say three things about him. Either he is a lunatic on the level of a man who says he is a poached egg, or he is a liar, or he is exactly what he says he is. It is nonsense, Lewis says, to profess admiration for Jesus as a great moral teacher and deny His claim to be God. For He is who He claimed to be—or He is a liar or a lunatic.

Now you and I, as thoughtful Bible students today, have to make a determination about Jesus. Considering His entire life—His miracles, His acts of kindness, the revolutionary things He said in the Sermon on the Mount—was He a liar and a fraud? Or was He perhaps a deranged fanatic? Or was He exactly what He said He was—the Son of God?

We're going to spend the rest of this book examining the evidence about Jesus. And I believe you're going to discover—and be thrilled as you discover—that Jesus was telling the truth! He was God. He was with God. And God sent Him to the town of Bethlehem in order that we might rediscover what God the Father is really like!

Jesus came to us as a Messenger from beyond the stars, to a society He knew would kill Him in the end. He came here with Calvary fully in His sights—because He had a message about God that couldn't wait any longer.

Let's take a side excursion to the town of Jericho, the hometown of a man named Zacchaeus. Zacchaeus was "a wee little man, a wee little man was he." I can remember when my two daughters, Debbie and Rebecca, were just little girls in church singing that song. And the rest of the song says that little Zacchaeus climbed up in a sycamore tree, "for the Lord he wanted to see."

But now, a bit of inside information not shared in that kindergarten song. What kind of a man was Zacchaeus? The Bible tells us he was a tax collector. You can read the story in Luke 19.

Even today some people make jokes about those who work for the IRS. But tax collectors in Jesus' day not only had a bad reputation—they had a well-deserved bad reputation.

You see, Zacchaeus had gotten rich through his tax collecting. Through out-and-out corruption, graft, taking three and four times as much as was fair, he had lined his pockets with the gold of Israel's poorest citizens. Worst of all, he had done it all in the name of the despised Roman government. No wonder Zacchaeus was not just hated, but hated as "the chief of sinners."

And Jesus, coming down the road, looked up into the branches of that sycamore tree, where Zacchaeus, all four-foot-ten of him, was perched, expensive Internal Revenue Service robe and all.

As all the disciples and Pharisees and taxpayers watched with great interest, Jesus looked up and said, "Zacchaeus, you come down! I'm going to your house today."

And at that moment, the whole watching universe learned something about God. Jesus called Zacchaeus by name. He wanted to be with him. He wanted to spend time with Zacchaeus and heal him from his sickness of greed and corruption. Let me state it clearly: *Jesus loved Zacchaeus.*

Jesus loved one of the lowest sinners on the totem pole. And if everything Jesus said was true, it meant that God loved Zacchaeus, as well. And it means that God loves every sinner.

Let's travel a few miles to the city of Tiberias for one more special glimpse of this God who loves sinners. Tiberias is a popular resort on the southwestern shore of the Sea of Galilee. Three miles north of Tiberias was the ancient town of Magdala, for which Mary Magdalene was named. Mary's sister, Martha, and her brother, Lazarus, lived far away in Bethany, a village just outside Jerusalem.

To make a long story short, Mary had gotten herself into trouble back home, and perhaps to save the reputation of her family, she moved to Magdala. Unfortunately, more trouble was waiting for her there.

Now Tiberias was off limits to Jews. You see, in building the city,

King Herod had desecrated a graveyard, which made the site unclean according to Hebrew law. Despite Jewish protests, Herod refused to abandon his construction of the city, so he had to populate it with non-Jews, many of them soldiers.

So here was a city full of Roman soldiers. And Mary was a prostitute. That's how she made her living. I can just picture her in the early light of dawn walking home along the seaside road between Tiberias and Magdala, her head hung in shame, trapped in sin without hope for a better life.

Then came Jesus. A Man who loved her in a different way. Jesus looked at Mary's scars and gaudy makeup and purse filled with money from customers—and He saw a child of God. Jesus reached out to Mary with pure, loving intentions. He won her heart back to wholeness with God.

You remember the story, one of the greatest in all the Bible, how Mary came to a feast where Jesus was eating. Suddenly the room was filled with the aroma of expensive perfume, the finest money could buy, as Mary showed Jesus how grateful she was that someone really could love her after all.

Yes, Jesus loved a sinner named Mary. What's more, He gave her a new life; He set her free from those links to sin that she had been so sure could never be broken. And He was saying all the while, "God the Father is just the same."

I remember a series of presentations I once gave in Massachusetts. One evening a thirty-one-year-old woman named Marcia, an airline stewardess, walked in. And there in those meetings she found Jesus. Marcia was just overwhelmed with happiness. Afterward she wrote me a note, and it said something like this: "Dear Pastor Finley: How could I be so blind? How could I be so stupid? I sit here and ask myself these questions. I've been running for thirty-one years, looking for something. My philosophy was go, go, go. I've never been able to sit down and relax; I've just been running from place to place, taking pills to calm me down, pills to sleep, drinking a glass of wine, trying to relax."

And then she said: "Feeling so alone. I never understood what inner peace was! For the first time in my life, Jesus has captured my heart. I'm not alone anymore. He loves me! He died so I could be forgiven. What a shame I never loved Him before. Thank You, Jesus, for loving me. I'm so glad I'm not alone anymore."

The loving Christ had reached out and touched another life. But I have just one more example to share with you—from a familiar old hill.

It's on Mount Calvary where we see the greatest of all demonstrations that God loves sinners. Imagine that Friday afternoon when those Roman soldiers took the hands of Jesus, held them flat against the wood of the cross, and then drove spikes through His flesh.

And Jesus, through the pain caused by His enemies, said this: "Father, forgive them; for they know not what they do" (Luke 23:34, KJV)! You can read it in your own Bible.

Friend, that's Jesus. Loving even that poor, foolish soldier holding the hammer and the bag of nails. Forgiving him! And God up in heaven, who *thinks* just like Jesus and *is* just like Jesus, loved that soldier just as much. The hearts of God the Father and God the Son beat as one in their love for every sinner who has ever lived.

You know, people through the ages have complained, "God, it's so hard to understand You. Why don't You show Yourself more? Why don't we see more miracles like in Bible days? Why can't You demonstrate with more signs and wonders, or send along another book easier to read than this old Bible? Do something big for us!"

And I can't help but think that God must want to say to each of us in reply, "I sent you My Son. That was the best I could do." Even God has nothing more that He can do. If seeing the life of Jesus can't help us to glimpse the love of God, then we're in trouble. Because giving Jesus was the best God could do. That was the final option. There's no bolder statement He could make. There's no grander gesture of love He could express. We either take Jesus as our picture of God, or we face a long, awful night of darkness and despair.

As we conclude this chapter, let me ask you a question: Don't you find that something changes in your life when you discover someone loves you?

Working for an international television ministry such as "It Is Written" often takes me thousands of miles away from my wife Teenie—as did this very trip to Bible lands. But even though I miss her, it's so good to know that she and the kids love me and that they'll be there waiting when I get home.

I can still remember the feelings I had when I found out that *she* loved *me*! I became a different man. I had new goals, new strengths, new loyalties because of the life-changing power of love.

At this very moment, I hope you've discovered something about Jesus. He loves you. And because God the Father is exactly like Him, God loves you just as much as Jesus does.

That kind of love is life changing. I know, because it's happened to me. And I'd be so thankful if it would happen to you as well.

Why not respond to that love right now while we say this prayer together?

* * *

"Dear God, we realize today that Jesus was Your gift to us. He came as Your representative, to reveal to us just exactly what You're like. To show us just how much You love us as Your sons and daughters.

"Thank You, Father, for the life-changing power of Your love. And today I pray for every man or woman who perhaps is sensing that love for the very first time. Make that love real in every life, I pray in Jesus' name, Amen."

3

The Blood Tells Its Story

Jesus the Sacrificed Lamb

Chapter 3
The Blood Tells Its Story

Imagine you are holding grains of sand from the arid deserts of the kingdom of Jordan. The sand of all these war-torn countries of the Middle East contains blood spilled through the centuries in a seemingly futile search for lasting peace.

I think sometimes what stories those bloodstains in the sand could tell us. The brief but bloody Gulf War in 1991—what tales of heroism on the part of Allied troops! A tragic river of blood from tens of thousands of Iraqi troops obeying the orders of their dictator with fervent loyalty. Blood from innocent children, teenagers, mothers, Kuwaiti and Iraqi alike.

And not too many miles from this spot, on a hill called "The Skull," blood mingles with the dust of two thousand years. The blood of one Man tells a story more dramatic than any other.

* * *

My film crew and I traveled on our *Discover Jesus* tour to the very spot millions of people believe is the moral turning point of all human history—a hill called Mount Calvary.

Just that word *Calvary* is rich with meaning to so many people. Songs, poems, sermons, emotionally moving appeals to return home to God—they all center around what happened on this hill back in the year A.D. 31.

The Bible tells us that Jesus "suffered outside the city gate" (Hebrews 13:12, NIV). And Calvary is indeed a place of execution just outside the walls of old Jerusalem. Some people think it was called "the place of the skull" because corpses and skulls were lying all around. But, more likely, it was a limestone hill that had the shape of a skull. Whichever, it was a place of torture and shame and agony—and, eventually, a bloody death.

I can't help but think that somewhere on that hill, buried in the dust of these many centuries, is still some of the blood that flowed from Jesus' hands and feet, and from those jagged wounds caused by the crown of thorns. Just a single drop of that blood—what a story it could tell!

Something about that blood changed the people who watched it being shed that Friday afternoon. Even that very day the blood was telling a story.

A Roman centurion, watching as Jesus' blood was spilled, was somehow moved to declare, "Truly this was the Son of God" (Matthew 27:54, KJV).

One of the two thieves crucified next to Jesus saw in that blood the identifying mark of a Saviour. "Jesus," he said, "remember me when you come into your kingdom" (Luke 23:42, NIV). That's a strange thing to say to a broken, bruised person who is only hours away from death on a cross. But somehow that blood had proclaimed a message to the dying thief.

And for so many others who either watched in pained horror that day or who heard the story later, even twenty centuries later, the blood of Jesus has had a kind of magnetic drawing power. There's something about the cross of Christ that draws men and women back to God. Jesus Himself, even before the crucifixion, realized this fact when He said, in one of the most meaningful prophetic statements He ever made: "And I, if I be lifted up from the earth, will draw all men unto me" (John 12:32, KJV).

Yes, more than all the great teachings of this Man, Jesus, more than the miracles and sermons and cleansing of lepers, it's this idea that His blood was shed for us on Calvary that quietly, gently, irresistibly attracts us to Him today.

I've been privileged to hold evangelistic meetings all around the world, including crusades in hardened Communist societies where thousands of men and women flocked to hear. And I can tell you that, without exception, it's when we begin to talk about the cross and Calvary that people's hearts melt. I've seen it happen time and time again.

I've had little grandmothers living in Gdańsk, Poland, and Budapest, Hungary, come up to me with tears streaming down their faces and just hug me and say in broken English, "Pastor Finley, I must know this Jesus." It's the cross that does that.

What is it about the cross that wins our hearts? What does it mean to say that Jesus died for us? How can someone else's death count for me and for you? These are the hard, deep questions of Christianity. But, friend, the answers are so satisfying, so life changing when we really understand the story that the blood at this ancient site has to tell us.

I heard a story once about a little boy who suffered a tragic accident, leaving him dying in the hospital. He needed an immediate blood transfusion in order to survive. Because he had a rare blood type, a matched donor might not be found in time. But his father, doctors discovered, had the same blood type. Dad immediately took off his coat and rolled up his sleeve. The nurse swabbed his arm and inserted the needle. As that life-giving blood flowed through the tube into his son's arm, the father said, "Take as much as you need. If you need it all, take it!"

I've thought a lot about that little story. It doesn't answer all the hard theological questions about Calvary, but it does tell us the greatest lesson about the cross: *The blood of Calvary proclaims the love of God!*

It's been said that Calvary is the brightest of Heaven's billboards, announcing the love of God. Not just Jesus' love for you and me, but the love of God Himself. Remember, Jesus was sent to us as God's gift! Remember that favorite verse—John 3:16? "For God so loved the world, that he gave his only begotten Son, that whosoever believeth in him should not perish, but have everlasting life."

But what did the blood of Jesus actually accomplish that Friday afternoon? Let's travel to a typical Jerusalem neighborhood as we look for an answer.

We're standing in front of some houses owned by families much like those in your neighborhood back home. Even with the ever-present danger of war and civil turmoil, moms and dads and boys and girls here try to live a normal life. Schools and jobs and household chores are the same challenge for these citizens of Israel as they are for each of us. As we focus for a moment on the role any parent in any country faces, I think we can discover the scarred history of the universe that led to the cross of Calvary.

Have you ever imagined what must have gone through the mind of God when the first faint stains of sin began to emerge in His perfect universe? We read about those initial whispers, the first rumblings of rebellion, in Isaiah 14:12-14.

> How you are fallen from heaven, O Lucifer, son of the morning! How you are cut down to the ground, you who weakened the nations! For you have said in your heart: "I will ascend into heaven, I will exalt my throne above the stars of God; I will also sit on the mount of the congregation on the farthest sides of the north; I will ascend above the heights of the clouds, I will be like the Most High" (NKJV).

I wish we had transcripts of all that went on during this heavenly conflict! Can you imagine a video record of this first battle in the great controversy between Christ and Satan?

It seems clear that the sin of pride sprang to life in the heart of Lucifer. For no reason! Inexplicably! This angel who had everything wanted more; he wanted to be like God Himself.

Now please remember something. God ruled over a perfect universe. Millions of happy angels had never heard of sin, had never had a jealous or unhappy thought. And surely there were holy creatures on other worlds, created just like our own two parents Adam and Eve, who also had no idea what sin was.

Then this beautiful and talented angel captain, Lucifer, came along earnestly speaking of a better way. A way of new freedoms, new, exciting choices, new liberties and opportunities for those who would follow him. This was the original New Age gospel, and it sounded so enticing.

Sin was a new idea, a brand-new force in the universe. No one knew where it would lead. Except God.

God knew that sin would kill anyone who took hold of it. Not because God wanted it to, but because sin, by its very nature, would separate a person from God, the true source of life.

Only God could see the end from the beginning. Everyone else—angels, other inhabitants watching this drama, even Lucifer himself—

had a question mark within their hearts. The question revolved around this central issue: Who was telling the truth?

I can imagine how God felt as He watched this tiny rebellion begin to grow and flourish. And how He felt when, despite His earnest warnings, a third of His own angels believed the enemy's propaganda and had to be sent away from Paradise.

Some people have wondered through the years: "Why didn't God kill Lucifer right then? Two seconds after that first sinful, questioning thought—*bam*! That's it! Think of the trouble spared!"

But can you imagine the confusion and fear that would have spread from one end of the universe to the other? A friend of mine describes this imaginary scenario:

Lucifer has sinned. God calls him in before His throne and destroys him on the spot. The next morning the other angels come around and ask, "Where's Lucifer?"

God says, "He's gone."

The angels say, "What's 'gone'?"

God answers, "I killed him."

"Killed him? What does 'killed' mean?"

"I destroyed him because he sinned."

And the angels say, "Sinned? What's that? What are You talking about?"

God says, "Don't you trust Me?"

And they say, "Well, we did—until now."

Can you see why this mystery called sin had to be allowed to demonstrate its own deadliness? God had to give His own enemy the opportunity to state his case for everyone to hear.

Lucifer's claims that God's government was unfair, that God's law couldn't be kept, that God's creatures could live happily apart from God's wise rule—these campaign statements had to be exposed for the lies they really are. And only time could accomplish that.

Try to visualize with me the original Garden of Eden. Adam and Eve, perfect in their newness of creation, are beginning life together in their virgin world. And God, like any loving parent who knows of danger ahead, tries to warn them about sin. In fact, it's one of the first things He has to share with them. In the very second chapter of

Genesis He tells them: "You are free to eat from any tree in the garden; but you must not eat from the tree of the knowledge of good and evil, for when you eat of it you will surely die" (verses 16, 17, NIV).

"If you sin, you will die." I'm sure God said those words as earnestly and with as much urgent love as He could convey. The price for sin was death. That warning is driven home to us from both testaments of your Bible and mine.

But let me ask you a question. Can you imagine God in heaven consulting with His Son Jesus, and saying, "Let's pick a penalty for Adam if he eats the fruit. What should it be?" They discuss this for a few moments and then say to themselves, "Let's have it be death!"

Or suppose they ask each other: "What should be the punishment if someone tells a lie? Death! If one of Adam's children should steal something? Death! If someone should commit adultery someday? Death!" Did God arbitrarily pick death as His punishment of choice for every sin, large and small? That seems harsh, doesn't it? Harsher than you and I would ever be with our own children.

There have been times that my wife Teenie and I have talked together after our children were in bed, discussing, "How should we handle this little problem or that failure?" We've tried to be simultaneously loving and firm in our discipline, but we certainly didn't choose death!

Let me tell you something. I believe that God in His wisdom knew from the very beginning that every sin, even a small one like eating from a tree you were told to stay away from, *would lead down a path* that would end in death. Only God, in all the universe, had the divine perspective to know the deadly nature of sin, to know that one sin leads to another to another to another. Until one day you're weeping at the cemetery.

You and I, as moms and dads, sense this. "What's wrong with one marijuana joint?" your seventh-grader asks. You and I know the deadly spiral of drug abuse, in which one experiment takes a kid to another, and that chemical adventure leads to a third. And then addiction, and crime, and one day we parents are sitting in the front row of a funeral chapel, wishing we could have found better words to communicate the deadly nature of sin.

It's the same with adultery. One whispered exchange can lead to a meeting that shouldn't have taken place. Then an overnight adventure, followed by lies to family and friends. Before you know it, two homes are shattered.

In today's AIDS-infected world, it's plain enough at last that some of our choices are going to lead to death. Not because God arbitrarily made death the penalty for every imaginable sin, but because that's just the deadly nature of sin itself. It grows. It takes over. It leads you step by step away from God. And being away from God, the source of all life, is nothing but the absence of life.

And all God could do was to warn us!

I appreciate the plain way Paul lays it on the line for us in his letter to the Romans. "The wages of sin is death" (Romans 6:23, KJV). That's plain speaking!

The *wages* of sin. The *eventual end* of sin. The *natural result* of sin. Only God could see it. And only God was telling the truth as clearly as He possibly could!

Of course, we all know the story of that first sin. Adam and Eve failed to trust God's plan for them. They didn't fully believe His warnings about sin. They took that first step away from Him, that first step, which inexorably leads to all the other steps.

But they didn't die! Not right away. Again, we see God's deep wisdom. Imagine the reaction around the universe if Adam and Eve had fallen dead on the spot the day they first sinned. Think of the fear that would have swept from one corner of creation to the other.

The message "*God* kills!" would have been plain for everyone to see. But the truth—"*sin* kills!"—would have remained a mystery.

God has never been interested in ruling a universe of beings who are terrified of Him, so He allowed time to pass in order that men and women could see that the enemy was sin itself. Adam did die 930 years later. By that time, the universe had witnessed murder, lying, stealing, adultery, and all the rest. Even after just a few generations, sin's deadly nature was already becoming painfully evident. In fact, as we explored in the previous chapter, by the time of Noah, sin was such a deadly virus that God had to step in as an act of kindness and call a temporary halt. It was an act of mercy for God to end some lives before sin itself did it in a much more cruel and evil fashion. And the universe watched that too.

Well, six thousand years have passed, and every single human being born on this planet has come under the curse of sin. You're reading words right now penned by a sinner. The Bible tells me, "Mark Finley, you're a sinner. Everyone in your 'It Is Written' viewing audience is a sinner." We've all fallen under the deadly spell of sin. Let's read the straight testimony from Scripture itself: "All have sinned, and come short of the glory of God" (Romans 3:23, KJV).

All have sinned. There you have it. I'm grateful that the Bible tells us the truth—even when it's painful. That's the only way we can discover what we need and then proceed to take hold of the solution our loving God has provided.

Can you begin to sense God's great dilemma? Human beings He loved with an infinite love had fallen victim to a power they could not understand, swept up by an enemy's intriguing lies. But tragically, this mystery called sin carried its own unavoidable penalty of death.

What would you, as a parent, have done?

We know the story of what God did. He sent His own Son to be born in Bethlehem so that He could go on to Calvary and fulfill Heaven's plan to resolve the great problem of sin.

Starting right in the Garden of Eden, on the tragic day when Adam and Eve first tasted the fruits of sin, God explained that plan. An innocent lamb died that day, representing Jesus, who would come down in all His perfection, and Himself bear that penalty of death. He would take on Himself the inevitable curse of sin before a watching universe so that sinners who chose to do so could accept that gift and live.

But perhaps a question has come to your mind. "Why does *anybody* have to die? God is God; He makes the rules. He can do as He pleases! Why couldn't sin simply be forgiven? Was Calvary really necessary?"

Those are questions many earnest Christians are wrestling with today. The great "Why" of Calvary.

Consider it with me. What would have happened if, following Adam's sin, God had simply swept it away and said it didn't matter? What would the watching universe have concluded?

For one thing, they would have been deceived about the deadly nature of sin. Adam and Eve would have continued down the path of sin, eventually destroying themselves and their descendants. All of us would have learned the hard way that departing from God's law into sin is guaranteed death.

To overlook sin would also have given the enemy an assured victory. "God's law can't be kept!"—that was Lucifer's challenge. "Living apart from God—in sin—will lead to greater happiness, not death!" We would have discovered too late the falseness of these satanic suggestions.

To overlook sin would have made God, not Satan, the liar. But neither could God simply let you and me reap the natural results of sin; that was a heartache greater than our loving God could bear. So Jesus came. In fulfillment of all the Old Testament sacrifices, He came. In fulfillment of countless Old Testament prophecies, He came to this earth and did what those prophecies said He would do.

When you've finished reading this chapter, why not take your Bible and quietly read through all of Isaiah chapter 53? This beautiful "Messiah" chapter foretells—hundreds of years in advance—the arrival of the Lamb of God. Read with me these three magnificent verses:

Surely he hath borne our griefs, and carried our sorrows: yet we did esteem him stricken, smitten of God, and afflicted. But he was wounded for our transgressions, he was bruised for our iniquities: the chastisement of our peace was upon him; and with his stripes we are healed. All we like sheep have gone astray; we have turned every one to his own way; and the Lord hath laid on him the iniquity of us all (verses 4-6, KJV).

Maybe at Christmas you've treasured those great choruses from Handel's *Messiah*, in which these words in music penetrate and touch your heart. Friend, that's why Jesus came to this earth—to pay that price for sin that you and I owed.

In old Jerusalem there still stands today a sobering sight: the Western Wall erected by Herod. The Western Wall, or Wailing Wall as it is sometimes called, is the Jewish people's holiest shrine. After Titus destroyed the temple in A.D. 70, that section of the wall was all that remained. Jews have flocked to it for centuries to mourn the loss of their temple and to pray. Hundreds of prayers ascend from this wall every day, petitioning God, even now, to send the all-powerful Messiah to deliver His people of Israel.

May I open my heart to you? I look at this scene, and I think to myself: what a heartbreaking tragedy! The Messiah *has* come! The Lamb of God came here two thousand years ago and paid that monumental price, but the great majority of Israel never recognized Him.

Jesus came to earth to pay sin's penalty of death. The pure, sinless, perfect Son of God was the only One who didn't owe that penalty for His own sins. So in the eyes of a watching universe, He gave His life for ours, and that was payment enough—in fact, more than enough—for this entire world's experience of sin.

Consider this as well, coming from a God who values truth and revelation so highly. The death of Jesus on the cross revealed dramatically and swiftly the sure results of sin. Rather than let this planet lurch on for tens of thousands of years toward inevitable extinction, the Son of God took our sins upon Himself. Your sins, my sins—everyone's sins going right back to Adam and Eve.

In thirty-three short years, sin had done its work to completion. The Son of God was dead. The entire experiment of sin was telescoped into thirty-three dramatic years, culminating on Mount Calvary on a Friday afternoon.

Yes, friend, Calvary had to happen. Remember that in the beautiful Garden of Gethsemane, Jesus Himself pleaded with the Father: "If there's any other way to save humanity, let this cup pass from Me." But there was no other way, and with those magnificent words, "Thy will be done," Jesus set about the business of saving the lost children He and His Father loved with an everlasting love.

Never forget that the cross pays the full penalty for sin. Never forget that the cross reveals—for the entire universe to see—that sin is deadly and that sin itself is the destroyer of human beings. But most of all, never, never forget that the cross shows us God's love!

That's the message of the blood! "God so loved the world, that he gave his only begotten Son" (John 3:16, KJV). If you believe the truth of that grand Bible verse, then the blood of the Lamb Jesus Christ can have a power in your life right now as we pray together.

* * *

"Father in Heaven, we thank You today for the blood of Jesus that saves. We thank You for Your truthfulness mingled with Your infinite love. And today we're touched by the realization that Calvary was the centerpiece of

Your plan from the very beginnings of this Great Controversy, which Jesus won on that unforgettable Friday afternoon.

"Lord, Your gift of Jesus on the cross has such drawing power. There may be thousands reading these pages today who never really have had an opportunity or an invitation to accept the free gift of salvation that Jesus purchased at Calvary. But, Father, we invite them right now to reach out and say "Yes." "Yes" to the gift that is free—and yet purchased at such tremendous cost. Thank You, Father. We pray in the name of Jesus the Lamb, Amen."

4

A King in the Barn

Jesus Our Example

Chapter 4

A King in the Barn

The date was May 29, 1917. Brookline Hospital in Massachusetts. A young woman named Rose gave birth to a baby boy. He looked just like the other babies squirming in the nursery that day. Mom and Dad, with their high hopes, thought it over and then decided to name him John.

The tag on his little ankle probably read "Baby Boy, Kennedy." Forty-three years later, John Fitzgerald Kennedy became the thirty-fifth president of the United States. Less than three years after he was inaugurated, the life that began in a Massachusetts delivery room ended just as abruptly on Elm Street in Dallas, Texas.

Or consider another starry-eyed young mother named Klara. Her little baby son came squealing into the world on April 20, 1889, in the town of Braunau, Austria. Not knowing what the future might hold for her precious little child, she selected the name Adolf. And Klara Hitler, too, held high hopes for her innocent baby boy.

* * *

In the small town of Bethlehem, however, it was a different kind of birth. No hospital. No baby footprints stamped on hospital records. No doctors to attend the delivery and cut the umbilical cord and provide medical aftercare.

There was a mother, a young girl named Mary. However, she didn't have to ponder what her baby boy should be named. Heaven itself had already provided her with the name, Jesus—or Immanuel, God With Us. And she didn't spend time with her betrothed husband, Joseph, wondering what her little baby might be when He grew up.

Heaven's messengers had told her that as well. Baby Boy Jesus, born in Bethlehem, was born to be a king, a king who would ransom His people on a nearby hill.

Have you ever stopped to think that when Jesus was born, there was blood? There was pain and pushing and a placenta—just as in any other birth on this planet. The Son of God came into this world as a very real human baby. In fact, eight days later there was the usual circumcision ceremony. Jesus was a very real little baby boy!

We've been talking together during this *Discover Jesus* journey about Jesus as God's gift. About Jesus as the divine Lamb, Himself part of heaven's Godhead. And the Bible confirms this again at the time of Jesus' birth. Here in Bethlehem for the first and only time in human history, a virgin gave birth. Jesus, conceived by the over-shadowing of the Holy Spirit upon Mary, was the sinless Son of God.

Still, Jesus was a flesh-and-blood boy. In the town of Nazareth, He surely must have played and run happily along the dusty paths, just like the other boys. He must have climbed the sycamore and olive trees with His playmates. No doubt He engaged in lively suppertime conversations with Mom and Dad and His brothers and sisters.

The Bible lists at least four brothers of Jesus—James, Joseph, Judas, and Simon. Did you know that? Jesus' family was a real family, with many of the same struggles and joys as other families in these Judean towns and villages.

All through Jesus' thirty-three years of life, we find evidence that He was a very real part of the human race. He got thirsty just like anyone else, as we discover when He asked a woman at the well in Samaria for a drink. He got just as ravenously hungry as His twelve disciples. In fact, when He met the woman at the well of Samaria, He had already sent His disciples into the town to purchase food because He was hungry.

And Jesus got just as tired as you and I do after a long day of work. Don't forget the little nap He took during the storm on Galilee. All the frailties of human flesh were His during His stay on earth.

You may be wondering: "Pastor Finley, what does it mean to us today to discover that Jesus was human like we are?" Well, let me tell you what it means to me! Better yet, let me illustrate with one of my favorite stories.

Back in the late 1800s a priest, Joseph Damien, left his homeland of

Belgium to serve as a missionary to the lepers on the Hawaiian island of Molokai. For twelve years he faithfully worked among those poor victims isolated by their deadly disease. But it seemed that it was all for nothing. None of the lepers there seemed to care at all that he had left the comforts of home to try to win them to God.

Then one day he noticed something on his hands—little white spots. He also felt a numbness in his fingers. It could mean only one thing. He had leprosy himself, just like the people he had been trying to save!

A wave of horror washed over him as he realized his situation; now he was doomed to an early death just like everyone else in the leper colony. Before, he had been only an alien visitor, but now that he carried the same death sentence as everyone else, he was one of the people. He belonged with them.

With fresh determination, Damien renewed his ministry. You can imagine how quickly word spread that the foreigner had become one of them, sharing their death sentence. Hundreds crowded outside his cottage to express support and empathize with him. The next weekend at services, the chapel was packed to overflowing.

What made the difference? Joseph Damien had become one of the people he was trying to help. He suffered what they suffered. Their death was his death.

Those lepers could relate to Damien because they realized he could relate to them! All of a sudden, his words of guidance had new meaning. Now his example—his philosophy for coping with the scourge of leprosy—had something to say to their hearts.

And I'd like to suggest to you that we have a Saviour in Jesus who can relate to what we are thinking and feeling today. He understands our hurts because He's been through those same hurts Himself.

On TV, you and I have seen the space-shuttle astronauts wearing those million-dollar protective spacesuits to shield them from the hostile elements of their new environment. But listen, when Jesus came to earth, He didn't come wearing a spacesuit to protect Him from human pain. He genuinely understands us because He genuinely became one of us.

I still remember hearing a godly preacher named Charles Bradford in front of a huge audience, saying, "I'm so glad I don't have a bionic Saviour who couldn't feel my pain. My Jesus didn't have eyes of glass;

He had eyes that could weep!"

Let me share a sentence from one of the world's all-time best-sellers, entitled *Steps to Christ*: "When Christ took human nature upon Him, He bound humanity to Himself by a tie of love that can never be broken by any power save the choice of man himself" (page 72).

Isn't that a beautiful thought? And the book of Hebrews contains some of the most wonderful statements you can find about the fact that Jesus identifies with His human family. Let me just list a few of my favorites:

Since the children have flesh and blood, he too [Jesus] shared in their humanity so that by his death he might destroy him who holds the power of death—that is, the devil (Hebrews 2:14, NIV).

He had to be made like his brothers in every way, in order that he might become a merciful and faithful high priest in service to God, and that he might make atonement for the sins of the people. Because he himself suffered when he was tempted, he is able to help those who are being tempted (Hebrews 2:17, 18, NIV).

We do not have a high priest [Jesus] who is unable to sympathize with our weaknesses, but we have one who has been tempted in every way, just as we are—yet was without sin (Hebrews 4:15, NIV).

I especially like that mention of sympathy. In the beloved Christian hymn "What a Friend We Have in Jesus," don't you love the line that says, "Jesus knows our every weakness; take it to the Lord in prayer"?

Hebrews 4:15 also mentions temptation. In the desert near Jerusalem we can picture in our minds that dramatic New Testament showdown between Jesus our King and Satan the Prince of Darkness. As Paul tells us, Jesus was tempted in every way, just as we are. After forty days of fasting and prayer in this wilderness, Jesus faced a moral challenge more overpowering than anything you and I will ever experience.

Can we truly say that Jesus has faced every temptation you and I have? Some young person reading this book may be facing a temptation to use cocaine or to steal cars. Did Jesus ever face those specific temptations? Others may be tempted to view images of sin and lust in some box-office smash hit at the local theater. Did Jesus ever face the temptation to attend an immoral movie in the neighborhoods of Nazareth?

In the Bible's thrilling account of Jesus' victory over His enemy Lucifer, we discover that He did indeed face the same *kinds* of temptations we face—all of them. Appetite is a physical temptation. Jesus experienced forty days of hunger. Every cell in His body cried out for food. His desire to eat after His extensive fast was a greater physical temptation than any human will ever face. His victory in the physical area assures us victory over all lusts of the flesh.

How about pride? A desire for self-glory? We read that the devil tempted Jesus to fling Himself from the highest walls of the temple as a misguided means of attracting attention to His noble cause.

Failure to trust God in difficult times? That's one of the strongest temptations we face today. And Lucifer attacked Jesus hard on this very point: "Worship me," he whispered, "and I'll give You an earthly kingdom the easy way. Without the pain of Calvary."

Three sweeping temptations, representing the very battles you and I face each day—and Jesus conquered all three.

You know, I won't pretend that I've always been a perfect dad. I've made many mistakes. But I've always felt that I was able to identify with the struggles of my three kids, because in most cases, I sensed that I've "been there" as well.

So often I've said to Mark Jr., "Mark, I can understand how you feel. When I was your age, I had something just about like that happen to me, and here's how I handled it." Or sometimes I've had to say, "Rebecca, let me share some wisdom that will help you avoid some of my mistakes." So my children know that Dad understands their problems. And Jesus, because He entered the trenches of our battles, knows all about our scars and our struggles with sin.

Imagine that you're standing with me on the edge of the Dead Sea. We've come for a specific reason. The Dead Sea isn't much of a place for swimming, but a lot of tourists do like to go into the water and just float. The salt concentration is so high that you can hardly force yourself beneath the surface. Not that you'd want to. A five-minute dip is enough for almost everybody.

The topic of swimming gives us a good means of examining the big reasons you and I, members of the fallen human race, so desperately needed a Saviour to come to this earth on our behalf. Suppose I'm at the swimming pool with my little boy (back some years ago, when he was about four). Suppose that for some reason—perhaps a bully does it—little Mark is tossed into the deep end of the pool. Let me ask you: What does he need immediately?

You're right! He needs a lifeguard to go in and save him. More than shouted instructions, advice, a reminder about the posted list of swimming pool rules, or anything else—at that moment little Mark Jr. needs to be saved.

In the last chapter, we discovered together that Jesus came to be that Saviour for us. He came as a lifeguard to rescue us from the deepest waters where we were doomed to drown in sin. He came to Calvary to redeem His lost children. Thank God for the saving, rescuing power of the cross!

But you and I need more than rescuing, don't we? The moment we accept the gift of Jesus on the cross, we enter into a saving relationship with God. We're covered, the Bible says, by the robe of Christ's righteousness. The righteous life that Jesus sacrificed on the cross becomes our life. That's the pure truth of the gospel, the very foundation of the more than thirty-seven years of "It Is Written" television ministry!

But then we need something more! Thank God you and I can be saved; thank God we *have* been saved! But now, we need for someone to show us how to live the kind of victorious Christian life that God had in mind when He created us in the first place.

Let's go back to our swimming pool and complete the illustration. You and I are drowning. The first thing we need is rescue. And we're grateful that Jesus has accomplished that. But now we need a Swimming Instructor to patiently reveal to us how to conquer that deep water. We need an example to show us the way.

And, friend, in Jesus we have that example! Jesus came to this earth as a heavenly King born as a human baby in a barn—so that He could show us in thirty-three short years how to successfully live in relationship with God.

And let me add this: Jesus was such a perfect example that His life completely shattered the claims of the enemy! Remember, Lucifer—Satan—had made some bold charges against God. "God's law is unfair," he said. "It's impossible for humans to remain loyal to God." Lucifer maintained that no one could live life in full and happy harmony with the ideals of God's government.

And for four thousand years it looked as though Satan would prove his point. Humanity had completely failed to live within God's framework. It *did* look as though perhaps something was faulty about the law of God—at least in regard to human beings.

But then Jesus came to Bethlehem. A King clothed in humanity. And as a human Man He lived in perfect harmony with His Father's law. Not only did He come to save us, but He came also to show us how we can achieve victory by adopting His methods.

Down by the Jordan River is all the proof we need that Jesus daily had on His mind the fact that He was our example. Have you read the Bible story of Jesus coming to these waters and asking His cousin John to baptize Him?

Think about it. Jesus was the one Person on the face of this earth who didn't need the cleansing symbolism of baptism! Baptism represents a washing away of sin, a burial of the old life of wrong habits and rebellion against God. Baptize Jesus? John the Baptist protested vigorously, as well he might. "I need to be baptized by You," he said, pointing out that he wasn't even worthy to untie the Saviour's shoes (see Matthew 3:11-14). But Jesus quietly encouraged him to proceed with the sacred ceremony.

And so Jesus, the perfect Lamb of God, was baptized "to fulfill all righteousness" (verse 15, NKJV). According to Jesus' own words, He was immersed in the Jordan waters to be a full and complete example for us in righteousness.

Let's take a short trip to the Mount of Olives, where Jesus so often loved to come with His disciples. Sometimes, however, He came to the garden by Himself. And it's really in those solitary moments that we discover Christ's power, His secret.

In John chapter 5, Jesus said something that might sound amazing to our ears. Listen: "I tell you the truth, the Son [referring to himself] can do nothing by himself; he can do only what he sees his Father doing, because whatever the Father does the Son also does" (verse 19, NIV).

"I can do nothing by Myself," Jesus said. Right away you and I may raise our hands in protest. Nothing? Jesus, who healed the sick and raised the dead and cleansed lepers and walked on water, said He could do nothing by Himself?

That's right, those are Jesus' own words. In fact, eleven verses later He spells that same idea out again: "By myself I can do nothing" (verse 30, NIV).

Jesus adds even more to this dynamic principle of Christian living. Let's allow Him to finish this puzzle, shall we?

Recall again that suppertime discussion in which Philip asked Jesus, "Lord, show us the Father," and Jesus quietly reminded him, "Philip, he who has seen Me has seen the Father" (see John 14:8, 9). Jesus went on to explain more about His source of power:

> Do you not believe that I am in the Father, and the Father in Me? The words that I speak to you I do not speak on My own authority; but the Father who dwells in Me does the works. Believe Me that I am in the Father and the Father in Me (verses 10, 11, NKJV).

Jesus, our Saviour *and* Example, came to this earth to show us this one life-changing secret: total dependence upon God. Jesus never used His own power, although He had plenty of power He could have used! Instead, He drew upon the power resources of Heaven. To heal the sick. To raise the dead to life. To gain the wisdom to teach and minister. Even for the power to resist temptation *and* to proceed through the darkness of Gethsemane and on to the cross of Calvary!

It's my earnest prayer that many of you, as you read *Discover Jesus*, have been saying "Yes" to God's invitation to accept Jesus as your crucified Saviour. But when you made that decision, almost immediately a question came into your mind: "What do I do now? What are my first steps as a Christian?"

Together, let's look at Jesus' example, shall we? The secret, we said, was His total reliance upon God. But how? What specifically did Jesus do?

Here on the Mount of Olives we learn the first step. The book of Mark reveals Jesus' strategy—His first line of defense against the enemy. "Very early in the morning, while it was still dark, Jesus got up, left the house and went off to a solitary place, where he prayed" (Mark 1:35, NIV).

Prayer was Jesus' first step. He linked up with His Father in earnest prayer. *Hours* of prayer. Luke tells us that there were times Jesus prayed all night. Think of it! Working all day until He was as tired as any man could be—and then praying all night! Work—and then pray—and then go and work some more. That was Jesus' way.

Jesus had a second source of power that serves as an example to us. *He immersed Himself in the Word of God.*

Jesus' prayer in John 17 provides insight into His sense of the vital importance of Bible study. Earnestly praying for His disciples, He asked His Father to "sanctify them [set them apart] by the truth; your word is truth" (verse 17, NIV). Jesus Himself spent long hours filling His mind with the powerful promises of Scripture. Jesus read the Bible. He read it often. In fact, if you look in a Bible concordance under the word *read* in the New Testament, you'll find reference after reference where Jesus is saying to an inquiring person, "Haven't you read in Scripture where it says this?" "Do you recall where God's Word tells us that?" Jesus was a walking authority on the Word of God.

In fact, when Jesus was faced with those three overpowering temptations in the wilderness, not only did He look to God's power rather than His own, but He responded confidently to each one of them with the same solid answer: "It is written" (see Matthew 4:4, 7, 10). Jesus had Bible answers for all of Satan's diabolical suggestions. "It is written," He said. You'll understand why I'm partial to that wonderful expression!

But please remember that God's Word didn't enter Jesus' mind by some divine miracle. Jesus had the saving words of Scripture in His heart the same way they can enter our hearts: by hours of quiet, thoughtful meditation in the Bible. That was Jesus' pipeline to the power sources of heaven.

Did you also notice that Jesus went into God's house of worship to do His reading? Here, too, we find Jesus as an example. *He fellowshiped together with the people of God.*

You know, in my many evangelistic crusades in Europe and the Far East, I've tried, through the Holy Spirit's power, to lead people to God. And one of the first things new Christian converts ask me is,

"Pastor Finley, what do I do now?" In addition to encouraging them in prayer and Bible study, I tell them, "Begin attending a Bible-believing, Christ-centered church that teaches the same truths you have been hearing in these evangelistic meetings." You may have watched the "It Is Written" telecast for years, or possibly you have studied the Bible truth for some time; it is now time to begin worshiping with God's people.

Listen, friend, I've been a pastor for many, many years. And I can tell you from the bottom of my heart—it's virtually impossible to maintain a successful Christian life hiding at home in the basement. God's people need to join together and draw strength from one another as together they draw strength from heaven.

I could use almost any travelogue video shot in Israel to illustrate my final point about Jesus as our Example. Jesus received power from heaven *in order to work among the people*. Jesus' power was an activist power; it enabled Him to mingle among hurting men and women and do the work of God.

So many Christians leave the path of righteousness because their faith has no expression in action. But the example of Jesus speaks volumes to us. For those three-and-a-half years, He worked tirelessly among the people who needed Him. Day and night, week after week, He preached and taught and healed and comforted. After being close to God in the mountains, He came right down to the plains and seashores, where aching men and women and children needed His healing touch.

So there you have it. Four steps that Jesus, the King of kings, followed to live as a human among us. He relied on God the Father's power through (1) prayer, (2) Bible study, (3) fellowship with the family of God, and (4) unselfish Christian service.

Let's return now to our picture of Jesus as a King who understands His people because He truly is one of them. A farmer put out a sign that said, "Puppies for sale." One day the newsboy, delivering the paper, got off his bike and asked, "How much do you want for your pups, mister?"

"Twenty-five dollars, son."

The boy looked kind of disappointed. "Well, could I at least see them?"

The farmer whistled, and soon the mother dog came running

around the corner, trailed by four cute puppies. Then another pup came limping around the house, dragging one hind leg. "What's the matter with that puppy?" the boy asked.

"Well, that puppy's crippled. The vet says it doesn't have a hip joint, and that leg will never work."

The boy reached into his collection bag. Pulling out fifty cents he said, "Please, mister, I want to buy that puppy. Here's my down payment. I'll pay you every week until the twenty-five dollars is paid."

"You don't understand," the farmer said. "That pup won't ever be able to run or jump. It's crippled forever. Why in the world would you want such a uscless dog?"

The boy paused and then slowly lifted up his pant leg, exposing a metal brace supporting a badly twisted leg. "Mister," he said, "that pup is going to need somebody like me who understands him."

Friend, Jesus knows all about your crippled heart. He was here among us. He tasted all the pain of humanity. Despite being a King of kings, He knows the very depths of your despair today. Everything in Him longs to hold you close and tell you, "I understand. My love for you goes beyond human understanding. I want to call you Mine."

Wherever you are today as you read these words, Jesus knows you. He knows *you*! The president or the leader of your nation may not know or care who you are, but Jesus, the King of the universe, knows and loves you right now. Read these wonderful words with me from the classic book *The Desire of Ages*: "Every soul is as fully known to Jesus as if he were the only one for whom the Saviour died. . . . He cares for each one as if there were not another on the face of the earth" (page 480).

Thank God for a King and a Saviour like that! Won't you join me right now in thanking Jesus for being our Saviour and Example and Friend?

* * *

"Father, what good news it is to know that Jesus identifies with the struggles we all have today. There may be someone reading this page today, Father, who is experiencing pain and heartache. The loss of a loved one through death or divorce. But thank You that Jesus went through our trials and understands the kind of strength and comfort we need.

"Lord, help us to pattern our lives after Jesus, our Example, today. And help us most of all to seek Your kingdom as He did—by trusting daily in Your power. For we ask it in Jesus' name, Amen."

5

Showdown at Sundown

Jesus, Lord of the Sabbath

Chapter 5

Showdown at Sundown

It was an emergency operation—a delicate piece of surgery. But in the late afternoon hour it was also a desperate race against time.

The surgeon was working with masterful precision, but everyone in the operating theater could feel the agonizing tension. Precious moments were slipping away, and the patient's life was hanging in the balance.

For decades, state law had dictated that no medical procedure, routine or otherwise, would be performed after sundown. Before this particular emergency procedure had begun, the hospital's legal department had informed the surgical staff that sundown this Friday evening would be at precisely 6:25 p.m.

It was 6:23 now. The two nurses, green uniforms sticking to their perspiring skin, handed the chief surgeon the sponges and clamps he requested. One of them cast a fearful eye toward the large clock that seemed to glare down forbiddingly at the group.

"Hurry, doctor." The rhythmic beeping of the heart monitor lent emphasis to the younger nurse's whispered plea.

The police officer standing in the background took a step toward the desperate trio. "You folks have two minutes."

The surgeon glanced at the clock again, then, with a shake of his head, looked toward the window. "There's no way!" he snapped, his voice raspy with fatigue. Even through the heavy drapes, he could see the last vestiges of disappearing sunlight.

He completed one final suture and turned to the head nurse. "Get ready to reconnect."

The nurse took one step toward the heart machine and found the state officer blocking her path. "I'm afraid that's it," he said evenly. "Please step away from the table."

"He'll die!" Rage flashed in the young woman's eyes as she tried to reach past him for the switch that would preserve the human life hanging in the balance. "Just a few more minutes!"

"I'm sorry." His arms folded across his powerful chest, the policeman glanced toward the draped window, as if to transfer blame to the setting sun. "Rules are rules."

The surgeon stood motionless at the operating table, helplessly watching his handiwork. It was only moments before the even, regular blips of the heart monitor began to sputter, then flutter almost graciously into oblivion. A steady, deathlike hum filled the room.

"I'm sorry," the officer said again, his tone more apologetic this time.

"Yeah." With weary sarcasm, the surgeon pulled off his mask and flung it down at the police officer's gleaming black boots. He looked once more at the two nurses, his eyes filled with pain, before leaving the operating room.

* * *

What you just read was a little dramatic piece of fiction. At least I hope it is fiction! If I'm ever in the hospital for emergency surgery, I hope those doctors and nurses just keep right on working on me until they're finished—no matter what time of night or day it may be.

But you know, in Jerusalem back in Jesus' day, that little vignette might not have been too far from the truth.

It happened one Sabbath morning, which, as you know, God's people in Bible times observed from sundown Friday evening until sundown Saturday evening. So it was a Saturday in the synagogue. And Jesus, as was His custom, was worshiping together with the rest of the believers. In fact, He was teaching on this particular Sabbath.

You can read this showdown story in Luke chapter 6. A man whose right hand was shriveled was in attendance, and Jesus' loving, healing heart was touched by his great need. But also seated in that synagogue were the Pharisees and the teachers of the law. Just watching, every one of them, to see if Jesus would break the Sabbath regulations by healing the afflicted man. That kind of work on the sacred Sabbath hours was absolutely forbidden.

Can you picture the scene? Just as dramatic in its own way as the operating-room scenario I just described. A man who needed healing was caught between two forces: the loving, healing power of Jesus and the rules of proper Sabbath observance.

Jesus sensed full well what was at stake. He knew the hearts of those Pharisees. And He realized that to heal this man on the Sabbath day would bring Him one step closer to His own execution day.

But Jesus didn't back away. In fact, He heightened the drama in order to make a point. He said to the man, "Get up and stand in front of everyone."

Then Jesus turned to those watching and asked them a question: "I ask you, which is lawful on the Sabbath: to do good or to do evil, to save life or to destroy it?" (Luke 6:9, NIV).

There was no answer. Then Jesus, with heaven's courage flashing from His eyes, said to the man: "Stretch out your hand" (verse 10, NIV). It was an electric moment, a Sabbath showdown. And the crowd gasped when they saw that shriveled-up hand miraculously restored to perfect health.

But some in that crowd didn't gasp. Instead, they grumbled quietly among themselves—and went out the back door to begin planning for a crucifixion.

Friend, what's going on here? Why had this issue of the Sabbath become such a blazing point of contention? How important a question is it anyway? Does Jesus' own view of the Sabbath have any relevance to men and women living in the 1990s?

Come join my little tour group as we journey to the Garden of Gethsemane to try to imagine something of the splendid glory of the original Garden of Eden. God the Father and Jesus His Son have just finished creating a brand-new world. Everything is perfect, including two beautiful new human beings, all wide-eyed in their fresh innocence. Adam and Eve—our first parents.

And do you know what was the first thing Adam and Eve did? They celebrated the world's first Sabbath together. You can read it in Genesis 2:2, 3:

> By the seventh day God had finished the work he had been doing; so on the seventh day he rested from all his work. And God blessed the seventh day and made it holy, because on it he

rested from all the work of creating that he had done (NIV).

We can make a list of several things God did on that first Sabbath. He rested on that seventh day, He blessed it, and He made it holy.

Now a question comes to our minds. Why would God rest? Even after six long and wonderful days of creating our world, was He tired? Was Jesus burned out and fatigued, needing a break so that He could collapse in the nearest chair?

I think we know better than that. Doesn't it seem more likely that God set aside that seventh day as a time for His two created children to rest and fellowship with Him?

Of course, Adam and Eve weren't tired either. They were only minutes old! But God, in His infinite wisdom, could look down through the pages of history and see the frantic pace the human race would adopt. That very first week of creation, God's kind heart put in place a resting time when He and His people could come together for a special twenty-four-hour haven of love and enjoyment.

So on the *second* page of the Bible we see the purpose of the Sabbath. Not for God's rest, but for ours. In fact, Jesus confirmed this point when questioned by the Pharisees. These religious leaders had criticized Jesus' disciples for walking through the grain fields and picking a little bit of grain to eat during the Sabbath hours. What did Jesus say in response? "The Sabbath was made for man, and not man for the Sabbath" (Mark 2:27, KJV).

From the very first week of creation, God had in mind a day of delight and spiritual refreshment for human men and women like you and me. In fact, the Sabbath is an eloquent statement to me of a God who actually comes searching after us, eagerly seeking time with us every week.

Let me share with you a little confession story. During my freshman year in college, I began to notice a pretty girl named Ernestine. Teenie, her friends called her. Our relationship was pretty casual during that first year, but during our sophomore year it began to get a little more serious. Unfortunately, she was living off campus, and I began to sense that I was facing quite a bit of competition.

Some interesting things began to happen. I was a jogger, and it just so happened that my newest jogging route went right by her house. Then, just by sheer coincidence, day by day when she'd come out of classes, I'd happen to be walking by. She worked in the college gym, and for some reason I always seemed to be practicing basketball during the hours she worked.

And, you know, this little string of coincidences just kept growing. Every time she went for a meal at the cafeteria, there I was, walking in the front door at the same time. In fact, right about that time I got bored with English Literature and decided to switch over to American Literature instead. Wouldn't you know it? She happened to be in American Lit—which made it convenient for us to study together in the library every evening.

Can I tell you something? It's no coincidence that Teenie has been a wonderful wife to me for twenty-five years! I'm willing to acknowledge it openly here—I pursued her. And God, through the gift of the Sabbath, has been pursuing His people since the beginning of time. Eagerly longing for fellowship time with you and me.

Now let me ask you to think seriously with me for a moment, with a detective's mind. We're here, let's say, in the Garden of Eden, where God has just set up this wonderful weekly time of friendship. Six days every week Adam and Eve—and maybe someday a flock of children and grandchildren—will work together and play together and build their homes and livelihoods. But every seventh day, every Sabbath, they'll put aside everything else and spend twenty-four glorious hours with their Friend and Creator. Every week they'll enter the sacred hours of Sabbath rest and learn to know and love their God more fully.

Now imagine with me. If you and I are part of the enemy's forces—Lucifer and his angels—how are we going to feel about this idea of the Sabbath? How are we going to respond when we see Adam and Eve spending glorious hours with God once a week, week after week?

We know the answer immediately. If we were part of Satan's forces, we would attack this concept of Sabbath rest any way we could! One way or another, we would have to destroy or pervert or sweep away this time of fellowship between God and His people.

Doesn't that make sense? In fact, as we read through the pages of God's Word and through the books of history, we can see a very detailed, almost diabolical, campaign to accomplish that very objective.

You know, whenever I'm faced with a theological question such as "Whatever happened to the original Sabbath of God's people?"—I ask myself this detective question: Who stands to gain if the Sabbath is destroyed or changed? Who would be the power behind such a move?

One of the "It Is Written" staff members recently told me a fascinating experience. Back in the mid-1980s, California citizens were scheduled to vote on whether or not to have a lottery. It was on the statewide ballot as one of the propositions. As you can imagine, the television airwaves were filled with commercials either extolling or condemning the concept of a state-sponsored lottery.

And my friend said, "Mark, it was interesting to see those commercials. Some of them suggested that the lottery was a great idea: it would raise money for our schools, it would decrease our taxes, it would be a painless way to solve our economic problems. These commercials almost made the lottery sound like a noble idea!

"But the 'No' commercials were just as persuasive that lotteries were a bad idea: gambling was an immoral way for the state to raise money, crime and corruption were bound to creep in, the poorest segments of society would be sucked into the dream of quick money."

Out of curiosity, my friend said to himself, "I wonder what forces are behind this lottery—on either side of the fence?" And do you know what he discovered? The "Yes" commercials were being paid for by the company that was bidding for the multimillion-dollar business of printing all the lottery tickets. And the "No" ads were being funded by . . . guess who? The horse-racing lobby in Sacramento. Apparently those race tracks didn't want lottery scratch-off tickets competing for precious gambling dollars.

Isn't it interesting—and ironic—to discover who is behind something? I would ask you again to consider carefully just who might be interested in destroying the idea that every seventh day you and I may fellowship with our Creator.

In our imagination let's travel to the foot of Mt. Sinai, where the voice of God thundered out across these plains with the Ten Commandments. You can find all ten, including the Sabbath commandment, in your Bible in Exodus 20. Some Christians today feel that those Ten Commandments were God's special statement just to the children of Israel. But God established the Sabbath as a gift to Adam and Eve back at the very beginning of Earth's history, as we saw a few paragraphs above. The Sabbath was meant to be treasured by all God's people.

You see, following centuries of slavery in Egypt, Sabbath rest had been largely forgotten by God's people. So God reiterated His Ten Commandments—not as something new or only for the people of Israel—but in order to remind His people and restore them to a relationship of weekly rest and fellowship in Him.

Let's look at this Sabbath commandment as expressed in Exodus 20. Perhaps it's been a while since you considered what it really has to say.

Remember the Sabbath day, to keep it holy. Six days you shall labor and do all your work, but the seventh day is the Sabbath of the Lord your God. In it you shall do no work: you, nor your son, nor your daughter, nor your manservant, nor your maidservant, nor your cattle, nor your stranger who is within your gates. For six days the Lord made the heavens and the earth, the sea, and all that is in them, and rested the seventh day. Therefore the Lord blessed the Sabbath day and hallowed it (Exodus 20:8-11, NKJV).

I like that positive challenge, don't you? Remember the Sabbath day. It's so easy to forget the Sabbath, and then it's just one small step before we forget the God of the Sabbath.

Did you notice how the Sabbath is forever linked to an understanding that God is our Creator? The Sabbath is a weekly reminder that He made us and that we owe Him our loyalty and love.

Every week the Sabbath reminds us to rest from our work and rest in God's completed work of creation. The Sabbath lets us know that whatever progress we've made in life, whatever projects we're working on, whatever deadlines hang over our heads—we can set them aside and rest, fulfilled and happy in Him.

Think of this. If people hadn't forgotten the Sabbath, there would be no such thing as a theory of evolution today. I've traveled through Communist countries, where evolution is an entrenched belief system. Even in the United States, it's a battle raging in our schools. Weekly Sabbath rest would have served to help us remember that you and I are God's creation.

Speaking of remembering, I'd like to offer you a unique gift. A few years ago I worked on a fascinating writing project dealing with this very topic. My research led me to some thrilling conclusions regarding the opportunities that exist for you and me today as we experience Sabbath rest. The book that came out of my study is entitled *The Almost Forgotten Day*. If you'd like to receive a complimentary copy for your own study, just write to me here at "It Is Written," and my staff will be happy to mail it to you. You'll find the address at the end of this chapter.

Now, let's travel back once again to the time of Jesus, shall we? At the site of the original Jerusalem temple, do we find that the Sabbath had been forgotten? "Quite the opposite," you say.

That's right. In fact, the Sabbath was being so rigorously observed, that people were suffocating on it. That sounds like a harsh statement, but there are innumerable painful examples to back it up. Let me share just one. Take an ordinary little handkerchief. Carrying it with you during the Sabbath hours was a grievous violation of the religious regulations of the day. A tiny cloth was an unnecessary burden, you see. But it was all right to pin that same handkerchief to your clothes— within reach of your nose, of course. Then it became part of your clothing, the rabbis said, not something extra.

It went on and on like that, with regulations and rules and headings and subheadings for every imaginable situation. None of them were found in God's Word; they had been created out of centuries of human tradition.

Can you see what happened? Again, let's ask that probing question: Who stands to gain when God's beautiful Sabbath rest is buried under a choking tangle of confusing and arbitrary regulations? Can you just visualize Satan quietly working behind the scenes to destroy the Sabbath from within? Throwing a heavy blanket of rules over the original concept of happy, life-restoring fellowship with God?

The ancient Pool of Bethesda near the Sheep Gate is a familiar tourist site today. Here Jesus found a man who had been an invalid for thirty-eight years. And even though it was Sabbath, and even though the "strenuous" work of healing was forbidden by what seemed to be hundreds of laws and bylaws, Jesus reached out a hand to that man and told him, "Get up! Pick up your bed and walk."

Of course, when that man picked up his tattered mattress and strode with his new strong legs toward the exit, he was breaking the Sabbath, too, by carrying a "burden." But not according to the wonderful Stranger who had just set him free from his physical bondage.

It seems that Jesus almost went out of His way to break the bondage of Sabbath repression. He came to sweep away the senseless regulations and restore the beauty of worshipful Sabbath fellowship. And who better than Jesus, the Lord of the Sabbath, to do it?

I'm so thankful for the bright new picture Jesus paints of the Sabbath! A day to do good—a day to be a blessing to others. A day to heal and restore and comfort.

Do you recall that little piece of surgical fiction at the beginning of this chapter? Let me tell you a quiet secret. I'm grateful for this picture of Sabbath blessing that God has shared with Christian doctors and nurses in my home church, the Seventh-day Adventist denomination. This church operates some of the finest hospitals anywhere—well-known medical facilities such as Loma Linda University Medical Center. And all around the world, Sabbath medical care is something very special and unique.

The Sabbath is a quieter, more peaceful day in Adventist hospitals. Any routine procedures that can wait for another day are cared for later. But when a little boy is injured in a car accident—when emergency strikes, as it inevitably does seven days of the week—those dedicated medical experts move into action. Following the example of Jesus, they breathe a prayer for God's wisdom, for His hands to guide their hands, and then they follow Jesus' example in extending God's gift of healing during the Sabbath hours.

Probably the most powerful lesson we can learn about the Sabbath is to be discovered in the hills near the town of Capernaum. Jesus retreated to this deserted spot for some well-deserved rest with His disciples. The only trouble was, word leaked out that He was there, and soon the spot wasn't so deserted anymore. Thousands gathered to receive spiritual nourishment. The hours went by, and those earnest people needed physical nourishment as well. You know the story. There were only five loaves and two fishes for those thousands of hungry prayer-meeting attendees—and no grocery stores nearby.

The disciples tried to send the people away, but Jesus wouldn't hear of it. "You don't have to send them away," He said. "There's enough right here for everyone to eat—go ahead and feed them."

The disciples were flabbergasted. "Lord, how? Five loaves and two fishes—there's no way!"

Jesus didn't seem distressed about their lack of resources. He told them, "What little you have, entrust it all to Me." And then what did He do next? He invited everyone to sit down and rest.

Now, I don't know about you, but when I'm hungry and there's no food around, the last thing I feel like doing is to sit down and rest. I want to rummage around for something to eat.

But in obedience to Christ, those five thousand men and their families all sat down to rest. They trusted Jesus. And you know what happened—the Bible tells us "they all ate and were filled" (Luke 9:17, NKJV).

What a picture of the Christian life! To stop our working and rest in Christ. And then—perfect fulfillment.

We're so tempted to work our way to heaven. But Jesus says to you and me today, just as He did to those hungry followers: "I have provided everything you need. Come, for all things are now ready."

Now let me speak directly to your heart for a moment. I've had so many earnest Christians ask me, "Pastor Finley, is the Sabbath still valid? Hasn't it been changed? Does God really care?"

Friend, if God felt the Sabbath was needed back in the quiet peacefulness of Eden, isn't it a hundred times more vital in our frantic, confused, traffic-snarled world today? Would God really have done away with it?

I get letters from thoughtful people asking: "Didn't Jesus Himself change the Sabbath?" No. There is no record of such a change—not on a single page of the Bible. On this absolutely vital question of a change in one of God's eternal Ten Commandments, the Bible contains nothing but silence—*deafening* silence. Jesus kept the Sabbath, and so did His faithful disciples and followers for long decades after His resurrection.

Sometimes even fellow Christian pastors telephone me and ask, "Brother Mark, don't you feel that to keep the Sabbath now—after Christ's victory at Calvary—is legalism? Aren't you trying to earn salvation by worshiping on the Sabbath?"

That's probably the most ironic question of all. You see, keeping the Sabbath involves *rest*. The Hebrew word for *Sabbath* means "to cease, desist, rest." Resting in Christ's accomplishments, trusting in His works rather than in my good works—that's the very opposite of legalism!

In fact, as we spend a few moments meditating at Calvary, consider that universe-changing weekend when Jesus died on the cross. Crucified on a Friday afternoon. Resting in the tomb on the Bible Sabbath. And then raised to life on Sunday with your salvation and mine guaranteed for all time. So when I rest on Sabbath, I honor Christ's glorious act of redemption on the cross. As He rested on the Sabbath, I rest, too, trusting in Him as my Creator and my Redeemer and Saviour.

There's so much more, but our *Discover Jesus* tour must continue. I would simply say to you—follow Jesus. Wherever He leads you. As He leads you to consider what the Sabbath might mean to you— follow Him. As you sense that He is searching for you right now, that He wants to enjoy weekly fellowship with you on His special, holy day—follow Him. That's all any of us can do, and that's all He asks.

I *am* so grateful that Jesus eagerly seeks time with His children every week. What a blessing those precious hours of fellowship are! Won't you join me in thanking God for that kind of Saviour as we pray together?

* * *

"Father in heaven, week by week we thank You for the gift of Jesus. And just now we thank You as well for the evidence in Scripture that You actively seek fellowship with us.

"Lord God, I know full well that the idea of Sabbath rest is so new to many earnest readers today. Bless them as they consider its potential in their lives. Give each one of us a willingness to say 'Yes' to the quiet promptings of Your Holy Spirit. Help us to be eager to follow wherever Jesus leads, for we ask in His name, Amen."

Note: If the Sabbath is brand new to you, this chapter may raise questions in your mind that are still unanswered. There is so much more I would like to share with you. I'd be delighted to send you a free copy of my popular book on the Sabbath entitled *The Almost Forgotten Day*. More than 100,000 copies of this book have found their way into the hands of thoughtful men and women. And I'm so grateful for the kind of people who are asking for it—searching Bible students who are open to God's truth. I believe you're that kind of person as well, or you wouldn't still be a part of this *Discover Jesus* experience.

Again, I have a free copy of *The Almost Forgotten Day* to share with you if you're interested. It goes into much more detail than I could in this chapter, and I can promise you some fascinating reading.

I hope you'll write! Just send your request to:

Mark Finley
It Is Written
Box O
Thousand Oaks, CA 91360

6

The Judge Who Faces Sentencing

Jesus Our Intercessor

Chapter 6

The Judge Who Faces Sentencing

It's a city described as "half as old as time itself." Archaeologists call it "Earth's strangest city." Petra stands abandoned in the lonely hills of Edom in the Middle Eastern country of Jordan. Known for its unique and mysterious rose-red walls of rock, this fortress empire remained hidden for a thousand years.

Three hundred meters up the rocky slopes of Petra, you can still see the altars and cult pillars where pagan sun worship was practiced. Where parents willingly gave their own children to be human sacrifices, slaughtered in a ritualistic river of blood.

In order to appease their angry god—the judge and deity they believed ruled over them—people in these ancient lands offered their young maidens as peace offerings. Often when an important new building was being erected, helpless, innocent children were buried alive in its foundation in order to win the favor of this tyrant in the sky.

Today we look back through the centuries, through the red dust of Petra, and ask: What kind of a god is this?

* * *

It's an everyday occurrence for a criminal to stand accused in court. It's another thing if his lawyer is himself dishonest. But the most unthinkable situation is if the judge is evil. Where do we turn if the judge—the highest power in our judicial system, the last person of last resort—is corrupt?

For those who are seeking after spiritual things, the question strikes very close to home. What if God, who is supposed to represent the very core, the absolute essence of righteousness and purity, is

Himself cruel and corrupt? What do we do then?

The Bible talks about God as a Judge. Verse after verse describes how He will pass judgment on all of Earth's inhabitants. Acts 17:31 is just one of many: "He [God] has set a day when he will judge the world with justice" (NIV).

In 1991 the whole United States watched in pained horror as a judge faced accusations. Seeking confirmation to the U.S. Supreme Court, the judicial candidate himself was judged by a Senate Committee, bar associations, the media, and millions of viewers. People everywhere were vitally interested in knowing if the judge could be trusted. How did he view people? How did he treat people? Were his motives and ambitions pure?

Those same questions are just as applicable to God. What kind of judge will He be? Do you and I need to dread the moment when our names are called?

You remember that I mentioned earlier one of Jesus' greatest objectives in coming to this earth. He came as one of us—to reveal the integrity of God's character. "Your Father in heaven is just like Me," He told His twelve disciples. "You see that I love you; the Father does too."

If God is truly a loving Judge, that's good news! If God is just like Jesus, then perhaps we can begin to breathe a little easier, don't you think? Let's consider this a little more.

Travel with me in your imagination to that sacred spot where Jesus spoke to His disciples for the last time. It must have been a very precious moment—sad and happy at the same time—as Christ said goodbye to His friends and followers. Picture the disciples watching Jesus slowly ascending from that mountain. If you or I step off a mountain, we go down! But the Son of God steps off a mountain and ascends to His Father. The law of gravity isn't as strong as the Creator of that law! The disciples watch Him go higher and higher until at last a cloud of angels shields the Saviour from their view.

Now remember, the disciples had Jesus' wonderful promise that He would return again. John 14:1-3 is a precious guarantee in your Bible. But I'm sure they were comforted to hear the good news once more from two beings sent by Heaven to share again the reassurance: "Men of Galilee, why do you stand gazing up into heaven? This same Jesus, who was taken up from you into heaven, will so come in like manner as you saw Him go into heaven" (Acts 1:11, NKJV).

But now the question we want to examine is this: What has Jesus been doing in heaven since that day He departed from this mountain? Almost two thousand years have passed. Is He really coming back? And what has He been doing in the meantime?

Central to these questions is the continuing issue of God as a Judge. What role does Jesus play in the judgment proceedings of heaven?

I'd like to share with you three things that Jesus is doing right now in heaven. And the first one we find in those verses in John we mentioned above—John 14:1-3.

Let not your heart be troubled; you believe in God, believe also in Me. In My Father's house are many mansions; if it were not so, I would have told you. I go to prepare a place for you. And if I go and prepare a place for you, I will come again and receive you to Myself; that where I am, there you may be also" (NKJV).

What wonderful truth is in those three verses! "Don't be troubled," Jesus tells us. Believing in Jesus and believing in God go together—that's good news. Jesus is returning—that's good news. And He's preparing a place in heaven for those who follow Him—that's good news too.

Right now I believe Jesus is preparing a Finley mansion in heaven—a wonderful place to live that is more delightful than any beautiful home in Jerusalem that we photographed during our recent trip. He's preparing a place, a home, for you and for every man or woman who chooses to give his or her life to Him.

Have you ever had this experience? You drive home after work on a cold winter evening in December. You come into the house and take off your overcoat; it's warm and comfortable inside with the Christmas lights glowing as you head up to the bedroom. But just as you turn the doorknob, someone inside calls out: "Don't come in here!"

"Why not?" you say.

"I'm in here wrapping presents!"

I suppose that's the one time we don't mind someone telling us to go away!

This wonderful Bible passage tells me that Jesus is in heaven getting things ready for His return. You can almost hear His faint call:

"I'm up here wrapping presents!" Don't you think He's getting eager for "Christmas day" to come? He's longing for us to be with Him forever.

What does it really mean that Jesus is preparing a place for us? It certainly doesn't mean He has a hammer in His hand and is nailing boards on our heavenly mansion. But it does have to do with nails and the wooden planks of Calvary. Jesus prepares a place for us by revealing to the entire unfallen universe that Calvary's cross is sufficient to save all of us. He prepares a place for us by revealing to the entire universe how we have responded to the claims of the cross. He prepares a place for us by presenting Himself as our lawyer in the judgment.

That is Jesus' function in heaven right now, and the Bible expands on it. Let's carefully consider the details of this important work, shall we?

Standing together near the old Jerusalem temple site, we can easily imagine the daily and yearly sacrifices that for centuries were offered here, pointing the children of Israel toward the day of the Messiah's arrival. Do you recall that there was always a high priest who stood as the representative of the people before God?

Once a year, on the Day of Atonement, that high priest would enter into the second compartment of the inner sanctuary—the Most Holy Place. There he would offer an atoning sacrifice before God for the sins of the people. The blood of a perfect lamb would be offered, symbolizing the cleansing blood of Jesus that makes provision for forgiveness of sin.Remember, now, the Bible tells us that Jesus serves today as our High Priest in heaven:

> Since we have a great high priest who has gone through the heavens, Jesus the Son of God, let us hold firmly to the faith we profess. For we do not have a high priest who is unable to sympathize with our weaknesses, but we have one who has been tempted in every way, just as we are—yet was without sin (Hebrews 4:14, 15, NIV).

That's one of the Bible's most compelling pictures of Jesus—our *sympathetic* High Priest. Whatever your weakness, Jesus understands it. Whatever temptations dog your footsteps, Jesus is familiar with them. Whatever heartache you feel at this very moment, Jesus has a sympathy that surpasses even a parent's tender heart.

In the same book of Hebrews, Paul gives us another glimpse of Jesus' role as High Priest. "Because Jesus lives forever, he has a permanent priesthood. Therefore he is able to save completely those who come to God through him, because he always lives to intercede for them" (Hebrews 7:24, 25, NIV). The familiar King James Version says Jesus can save "to the uttermost." Don't you like that? There's wonderful news for us in these verses.

But the vital point to notice is that Jesus as High Priest serves as our intercessor. Tell me, have you heard that word before? An intercessor?

If I intercede on your behalf, it usually means I go to bat for you. Maybe I represent you in a dispute at work. Maybe I go with one of my children down to the principal's office. Perhaps as a pastor I might intercede in a situation where a husband and wife are experiencing marital difficulty.

And here, just as the high priest in the earthly sanctuary interceded for the people, we find that Jesus is our High Priest in the heavenly sanctuary, interceding on our behalf, pleading our case. I can just hear Jesus saying, "Look at My follower, Bill. Father, he's accepted what We did for him at Calvary. He's taken time each day to nurture a relationship with Me. I want My sacrifice on Calvary to count for Bill."

Now, what do you suppose the Father says in response? This is where the Bible shares the best news of all!

If we take an Israeli taxi over to the Knesset, Jerusalem's government buildings, we can create an atmosphere in which to imagine God, the righteous Judge, listening to the earnest words of Jesus our High Priest. Are we to understand Jesus' intercessory work as attempting to persuade a reluctant God to let you and me into heaven?

Read with me 1 John 2:1. "My little children, these things I write to you, that you may not sin. And if anyone sins, we have an Advocate with the Father, Jesus Christ the righteous" (NKJV).

You may say, "Pastor Finley, that *does* sound like we need Jesus to persuade the Judge, God the Father, to let us be saved. Jesus the Advocate is on our side, but it doesn't sound like God is!"

And if you read this same text in the New International Version, it says this: "We have one who speaks to the Father in our defense—Jesus Christ, the Righteous One." Again, it almost sounds like heaven's judgment scene is one replay after another of "Jesus vs. God."

But let's not overlook the wonderful principle we've been discovering over and over here in the Holy Land. *Jesus and God are the same!* They have the same purpose, the same goals, the same desire that you and I be saved. God the Father is just as eager as Jesus is for you to inherit eternal life by accepting the gift of Calvary!

Remember our favorite verse? "God so loved the world, that *he gave* his only begotten son" (John 3:16, KJV, emphasis supplied). And 2 Corinthians 5:19 adds, "God was in Christ, reconciling the world unto himself" (KJV).

Let me say this to you as earnestly as I can. Don't ever allow yourself to have a mental picture of a loving Jesus pleading with a reluctant or angry God! I treasure that old hymn "There Is a Place of Quiet Rest." The refrain begins, "O Jesus, blest Redeemer." And what's the next line? "Sent from the heart of God." So many rich Bible passages reinforce this idea, such as this one in 2 Peter 3:9. "The Lord . . . is longsuffering toward us, not willing that any should perish but that all should come to repentance" (NKJV).

Let me share an experience of a friend of mine who had to take his fourteen-year-old daughter to traffic court. She had gone through a stop sign on her bicycle.

When they got there, the room was full of young people, all with nervous looks on their faces and impatient parents at their sides. Right at the appointed time, in came the judge. My friend said to me later, "My view of God was changed by that judge! He *loved* young people!"

The first young man, barely sixteen years old, had been cited for doing seventy-five miles an hour in a fifty-five zone. The judge talked very kindly to the boy, asking him, "Do you know what a collision can do to a young man going seventy-five?"

"No," the boy answered.

"Well, I do," the judge said to him. "I've seen it. I've seen young bodies pulled out of wreckage. Son, I don't want to see that happen to you."

Then it came time for sentencing. The judge looked down at him and said, "I'd like for you to attend traffic school for two days. Now, according to law, I have to give you a choice between traffic school and a fine, but I want you to select traffic school because that's what you need."

The boy thought for a moment and then asked, "How much would the fine be?"

The judge had a little smile on his face when he answered. "Five million dollars."

Everybody in the courtroom laughed, and the boy gulped and said that perhaps he could arrange his schedule to go to traffic school.

My friend told me afterward, "Mark, in case after case, that judge did all he could to help those kids. He was on their side."

Friend, can you see God in that light? When we see God that way, we read again the verse that says Jesus is our Advocate *with* the Father—and we understand that Jesus and God are working together, both of them defending us against the charges of Satan, the enemy.

Satan, you see, would love to deny you and me the joy of fellowship with God in heaven. But when he raises his accusations against us, God and Jesus together point to the blood of Calvary and agree together that every son, every daughter who has accepted that blood is counted worthy to be included. Together, they tell Satan, "Objection overruled!"

What a God! What a High Priest! Together, what a wonderful defense team!

There's a beautiful illustration springing from the heritage of justice in Old Israel. In those days, judges were not the impartial arbiters they are today. No, the judge was on the side of the accused, looking for every opportunity to defend and eventually acquit. Only when overwhelmed by the most clear-cut evidence would the judge reluctantly abandon the prisoner and pronounce sentence.

That's the picture of God I hope you can treasure in your heart today. He is working together with Jesus to save every man and woman He possibly can. God is eager to say "Yes" to Jesus' claims on our behalf. He's just not willing for you to be lost!

I've mentioned several times during this *Discover Jesus* saga the idea of the war between God and the enemy—the Great Controversy between Christ and Satan. And in a sense, it's God Himself who is being judged in the judgment.

Watching worlds have been looking on for centuries to see how God will resolve the sin problem. Has the death of Jesus on the cross really demonstrated how deadly sin is? Has it adequately proved that God's law and government are just as well as loving? How about God's dealings with men and women? Is He a fair Judge? Does He grant salvation carelessly or deny it selfishly and arbitrarily?

All the protestations and accusations by Satan die away as the universe sees how fair God is. How He has gone the second and third mile to make salvation available as a free gift to every person. And how He is eager beyond understanding that you and I accept that free gift.

Won't you come with me to the village of Bethany, where Jesus raised His friend Lazarus from the dead? We already have so much good news about Jesus to digest and meditate on, but please let me add just one more relevant fact.

What else is Jesus doing in heaven today? Friend, He's there to make His power available to you right now!

The same power that brought Lazarus out of a tomb in Bethany is still effective today. Jesus is the same yesterday, today, and forever—His power *right now* is yours for the asking. Administrations in Washington, D.C., change every four or eight years, but not in heaven! The same Jesus—with the same power—is paying close attention to your every need right now.

So often after meetings where I've spoken, someone will come up to me—perhaps a young person—and say, "Pastor Finley, are these just stories, or is Jesus real today? Can He help me right now?"

Yes! Over and over again—yes! He has power today that matches His power here in Bethany. And He has an interest in you personally, a deep love for you that springs from the same heart that loved Mary, Martha, and Lazarus two thousand years ago.

Let me tell you a story from my own childhood that illustrates the heart of a loving Father.

It was a hot summer afternoon in Norwich, Connecticut, and a group of us boys began a pickup baseball game in the backyard of one of my friends. We had a great time until about the third inning. It was my turn at bat. I got one of those hits every teenager dreams about. The ball sailed over the center fielder's head. It was going . . . going . . . GONE! Over the fence, out of sight . . . and through the neighbor's window.

I was horrified. I began to run—not around the bases, but home.

I'd better tell Dad before the neighbor lady called. Racing the phone, I sprinted for all I was worth.

Dad listened carefully to the news, then simply said, "Let's get in the car." Together we drove to the neighbor's house. He listened as I explained how I had broken the window. Then as I stood there wondering what would develop, I was amazed at what happened next. Dad spoke in a quiet, calm voice. "Mrs. Gerhard, I'm Mark's father. I'll take full responsibility for what has happened. He's guilty; he broke the window. But don't worry, I'll pick up the broken pieces and repair the damaged window immediately."

What an illustration of a loving God! Our heavenly Father assumes full responsibility for our failures. With His loving arms around us, He announces to the universe that He's willing to take upon Himself the full impact of the guilt of our sins. But there's still more. He picks up the broken pieces of our lives. He repairs the damage and makes us new again.

Has the guilt of your life so depressed you that you wonder if there's any hope left? Has your life been left shattered like some window smashed to bits? Do you need someone to pick up the broken pieces? Do you need a new start?

Our heavenly Father isn't a severe judge just waiting to condemn us. When we confess our sins, He puts His arms around us and announces before the whole universe: "This is My son. This is My daughter. I've taken the responsibility of their failures upon Myself. They're forgiven. I will repair the broken pieces of their lives so they can be a window through which the world can see the marvels of My grace."

God is eager to embrace you right now! To stand up for you as Defender and Healer! Wherever you are, whatever your need, Jesus is watching—and just waiting for you to ask. At this very moment, He's poised—ready to share His incomparable power. Can you feel it? Write this down and never forget it: "I can do all things through Christ who strengthens me" (Philippians 4:13, NKJV). Let His magnificent love surround you right now as we pray together.

* * *

"Father, day by day as we gain new glimpses of Jesus, we gain new glimpses of You as well. Thank You, Father—from the bottom of our

hearts—for the gift of Jesus Your Son. Thank You for sending Him as a gift from Your heart.

"Father, today we're so grateful that a place is being prepared for us in heaven. And we're grateful that You are together with Jesus in seeking our salvation. At this very moment we call upon the mighty power of Jesus—as vibrant and effective today as it was in Bible times—and we thank You for making that power available to us just now. In Jesus' name, Amen."

7

The Great War Is Over

Jesus the Triumphant King

Chapter 7

The Great War Is Over

They dropped out of the midnight sky over Lake Victoria, landed, and coasted silently down the runway toward the Entebbe airport terminal. There in the heart of Africa, more than a hundred Israeli hostages held their breath between life and death.

As the Hercules C-130s rolled to a stop, one of them dropped its tail ramp. Out came a black Mercedes limousine, along with two Land Rovers filled with commandos disguised as Palestinians. In the back of the limousine sat a bulky officer with his face blackened, impersonating the Ugandan dictator Idi Amin.

Now the commando team approached the terminal, led by the black Mercedes. The airport guards snapped to attention and saluted, recognizing Amin's personal license plate (counterfeited by the Israelis). The rescuers moved past the guards toward the hostages.

Inside the terminal, the shooting lasted a minute and forty-five seconds. Then came the triumphant shout of liberation: *Hanachnu Israelim* (We are Israelis)!

As the C-130s with their precious cargo lifted off into the friendly skies of freedom, some of the former hostages wept. Others sat in stunned silence. One woman kept crying out, *Moq Ness! Ness!* (A miracle! A miracle!).

And that it certainly was. The Israelis called their mission "Operation Thunderball," after the James Bond thriller. The commandos returned home to be hailed as international heroes.

* * *

Many of our longtime "It Is Written" viewers and readers will remember the above scenes as part of a dramatic telecast, "Thunder-ball From Israel," from George Vandeman's TV miniseries, *Show-down at Armageddon*. I wish Pastor Vandeman could have joined us for this entire *Discover Jesus* trip through the land of our Saviour. The subject of the second coming of Jesus has always been one of his favorite themes.

What greater moment can there be than that of deliverance? To be a hostage set free, a POW released, a prison-camp inmate rescued from a sentence of death?

I've been in many of the Eastern European countries so recently liberated from the oppressive bondage of totalitarianism. I've seen up close the joy in people's faces when they realize that war is over and their enemies vanquished. There's nothing like it.

You know, over the years so many missionaries have served the Lord under conditions of warfare and prison captivity. I wish you could read *Behind Barbed Wire*—a thrilling story of a Seventh-day Adventist missionary couple, John and Olga Oss, and their long years of detention in a prison camp during World War II. Along with many Christian workers of several different denominations, they struggled to survive under unbelievably oppressive circumstances.

Then one day the most beautiful sight in the world met their eyes. Huge American bomber planes flew right over the camp, dipping their wings as if to say, "Hold on! Rescue is near! The great war is over!" What a feeling to know that freedom had come at last!

And for us who are held hostage in a world of sin, rescue is on the way as well. The King is coming to set us free and take us home!

Let's take a final trip to the top of the Mount of Olives overlooking Jerusalem. Perhaps at this very spot, Jesus made some of His most startling predictions about the time you and I are living in today. When you watch the evening news, you're seeing right now the dramatic fulfillment of many of the things Christ prophesied would happen in the last days.

One of the most beautiful sights in all Judea back in the days of Jesus was the temple of Solomon. It was a huge, magnificent edifice, the glory of the entire nation. Enormous, almost pearl-white stones carefully piled one on top of the other created an image of lasting strength and solidarity. You can imagine, then, how surprised the disciples were when Jesus said to them: "Assuredly, I say to you, not one stone shall be left here upon another, that shall not be thrown down" (Matthew 24:2, NKJV).

"What?" I can just hear the disciples protesting. "The temple destroyed? Even these magnificent foundation stones thrown down? Not in a thousand years! Not in ten thousand!"

But this impossible prediction by their Saviour prompted the disciples to ask further: "Tell us, when will these things be? And what will be the sign of Your coming and of the end of the age?" (verse 3).

I find it so significant that these twelve disciples had the same interests as men and women today: What does the future hold for me and my family? Can I have hope for a better life beyond this one?

I've presented all kinds of public meetings: stress seminars, parenting classes, workshops on basic Christian living. But I suppose the best-attended programs are always those that deal with Revelation prophecies and end-time events. People are hungry to know about their future!

Only Jesus is equipped to reveal reliable information to us. Jesus, who was Himself the fulfillment of so many Bible prophecies, could foretell with pinpoint accuracy the events yet to come.

Why not take your own Bible and read through Matthew 24 and Luke 21? Both of these chapters contain prophecies—many of them with dual fulfillments.

Let me explain that a little bit. All through Matthew 24, for instance, Jesus gave information and warnings that applied not only to the soon-coming destruction of Jerusalem but also to the final destruction of the entire world. We can find meaning and counsel for both situations at the same time.

Now, let's open up our history books and see if these prophecies of Jesus were fulfilled in the short term. In the year A.D. 70, just a few decades after Christ lived here on earth, Roman armies advanced upon Jerusalem. The Tenth Legion occupied the Mount of Olives. Three other legions camped over on Mount Scopus and around to the west. The Roman general, Titus, prepared his forces to besiege the city. He pinned down the Jewish defenders by having the Tenth Legion bombard the Temple Mount with huge stones shot from catapults.

Interestingly, Titus, who was the son of the new emperor, actually had a reputation for generosity. Had the Jews surrendered to the inevitable, he probably would have treated them humanely. But they determined to resist, with a blind certainty that God was still on their side. Titus had no choice but to continue building the siege ramp against Jerusalem's wall.

With the first strike of the Roman battering ram, a loud cry went up within Jerusalem. You see, by the terms of ancient law, surrender had to be unconditional after the battering ram began its work.

An eyewitness account was recorded by Josephus, a Jewish general and historian who had made personal peace with the Romans. He relates in vivid detail the tragic events of Jerusalem's last days.

Titus had hoped to preserve the magnificent temple, but the Jewish defenders took refuge within its chambers. After they resisted all efforts to flush them out, a soldier threw a burning torch through a window. Soon the temple was a blazing inferno as the rich heritage of Jewish worship went up in smoke. After the flames subsided, the triumphant Romans offered pagan sacrifices on the temple property. As you can imagine, that was the last straw—the ultimate abomination.

So Jerusalem was besieged and the temple fell, just as Jesus had foretold—even to the point that not one stone was left upon another. You see, as the fire raged, gold and silver from the temple melted and ran between the stones. The soldiers pried those huge blocks apart in order to reap the bonanza. So it was that Christ's word was fulfilled in absolute detail.

After the fall of the temple, the Roman army systematically destroyed Jerusalem. Houses of the rich and poor alike were devoured in the flames. One of the most fascinating sites in Israel is the Burnt House, uncovered by archaeologists beneath the old Jewish quarter of Jerusalem. You can see the bones of an unburied hand and forearm, mute testimony to sudden death.

According to the records of Josephus, more than a million Jews died during the destruction of Jerusalem. But Christians throughout the city managed to escape. Almost to a person, they survived the holocaust of Roman fire. Why? Did they know something the others didn't?

Yes! They heeded a specific warning Jesus had given His followers that afternoon on the Mount of Olives:

When you see Jerusalem surrounded by armies, then know that its desolation is near. Then let those in Judea flee to the mountains, let those who are in the midst of her depart, and let not those who are in the country enter her (Luke 21:20, 21, NKJV).

"When you see Jerusalem surrounded by armies," Jesus said, "then it's time to get out! Instantly!" This was to be the signal for Christians to escape. And sure enough, events again transpired in a direct fulfillment of Christ's prophecy. Here's how it happened.

After the Jews revolted against the empire—but before the successful siege by Titus—the Roman governor of Syria, Cestius Gallus, marched his forces into Galilee. His army met with easy success and advanced south, conquering as it went. When he reached Jerusalem, Gallus ordered his soldiers to encircle the city. Winter was coming, however, and the army wasn't prepared for a long siege. After a failed attempt to storm the temple, Gallus suddenly withdrew.

The Jewish defenders seized their chance. Like hornets, they pounced upon the retreating Romans, chasing them all the way down to the Mediterranean coastal plain. In triumph they returned to Jerusalem, confident that God had delivered them.

But the Christians knew better. Jesus had said Jerusalem would be destroyed. He had told them that the encircling army was their sign to escape. And when the soldiers suddenly withdrew, the believers took their opportunity to flee as Christ had told them to.

You know, as we read these chapters of predictions, I'm so thankful that they not only point out the signs of what is coming on the world, but provide for our escape as well. There's more to these last days than destruction—there's also a Deliverer!

I like to tell my seminar audiences, "Don't focus on the crisis—focus on the *Christ* of the crisis! Instead of discovering gloom and doom in the Bible, discover Jesus the Rescuer there!"

Wherever you are today, I'd like to invite you to think with me about Jesus' promise that He will come again. In the previous chapter, I shared two of the Bible's clearest guarantees that Jesus will return. But there are so many more! Someone has counted 1,500 Bible references to the second coming. For every Old Testament text referring to the first coming of Jesus there are eight passages announcing His second coming. One in every twenty-five verses in the New Testament mentions the second coming of Christ.

When is He coming? Just like the disciples, we'd like to know. We'd like to somehow use Bible charts and calculators to figure out the day. But men and women through the years have had their hopes dashed and their reputations shattered as they ignored the Bible's plain words: "Of that day and hour no one knows, no, not even the angels of heaven, but My Father only" (Matthew 24:36, NKJV).

We're well advised to heed that text, aren't we? But we're equally well advised to read the signs in the Bible and look up and rejoice that the day of deliverance has to be near!

Jesus reveals to us more than twenty signs that His second coming is near. There's no one mega-event we can point to and say, "This is it!" Serious prophecy students aren't calamity howlers who say Jesus is coming this year or next year because of the San Francisco earthquake that rocked Candlestick Park or because some dictator just invaded his neighbor. Our eyes need to be fixed on the larger picture. And if we look around, we can see *numerous* signs in the world that clearly indicate that our Redeemer is coming soon.

Famines. Look around you. We stand on the brink of ecological disaster. Today four out of five babies are born in countries unable to supply their own food needs. Five and a half billion citizens of earth claw at one another for living space. India's total population exceeds 700 million—with 600 million of them malnourished. Tens of thousands have died of starvation in the sub-Saharan countries, with perhaps 70 percent to 90 percent of their cattle dead as well.

Wars and rumors of wars. Look around you. Just since 1960 we've had more than twenty-five major wars in the world. Vietnam. Iran vs. Iraq. Afghanistan. When the Berlin Wall came down, we were tempted to think a new age of peace had come. "Let's dismantle the military," many people said. Only months later we were swept into Desert Storm. And then Yugoslavia—brutal, bloody fighting in 1992! Every single year more than 180 billion dollars are spent on weaponry and armaments, getting ready for more conflict to come.

How about *earthquakes*? Let me say again—look around you. The disaster in San Francisco in 1989 was just *one-thirtieth* the magnitude of the Big One experts tell us is on its way. Earthquakes have increased dramatically in the last fifty years. Today more than three thousand major quakes are recorded annually. Earth's crust has destabilized since the secure days before the Flood of Noah. The Bible says our world is "waxing old" (see Psalm 102:26). Continental plates are shifting; geologic faults are sliding toward catastrophe. Imperceptible forces are at work under the ground, culminating in tragedy and ruin.

Lawlessness. Look around you. In the United States' recent political campaign, candidates on each side tried to out "law-and-order" each other. Build more prisons! Speedier executions! And all a sign that the end is closing in.

But the greatest sign of all, being fulfilled this very moment, we find in Matthew 24:14. "This gospel of the kingdom will be preached in all the world as a witness to all the nations, and then the end will come" (NKJV).

A new day is dawning, the Bible tells us. There will be one final burst of spiritual energy, as God Himself opens the doors so that good news about Jesus can be shared in lands where darkness has reigned.

Friend, I know this particular prophecy is true because I've stood in the very whirlwind of its fulfillment! In the summer of 1990 I stood waist-deep in a lake in one of downtown Moscow's most beautiful parks. What was I doing? Baptizing new Christians—while Soviet National Television approvingly recorded the whole moving ceremony!

Just a few months ago I was invited to preach nightly in the Kremlin Congress Hall, the former heart of atheistic Communism. For eleven straight nights the hall was packed! They *sold tickets*, and the place was sold out. What a hunger for truth! That's the most thrilling demonstration of all that God is moving to fulfill these final prophecies before Jesus returns. Totalitarian regimes have been swept aside! Atheistic governments have fallen! Despotic regimes have crumbled! Worldwide the doors are open for the proclamation of the gospel. There's a new spirit of openness "blowing in the wind." The Spirit of the Lord is touching the lives of millions in the former communist countries.

As our final moments of this *Discover Jesus* experience pass by, let's look at Him one final time, shall we? Think about why He came. Think about His gift on Calvary. Think of the price He paid for your forgiveness and salvation.

Friend, would He pay the price and then not come to claim His prize? If my son Mark Jr. were to pick out some boyish dream and make weekly payments until it was paid for, do you think he wouldn't then go down to the store and pick up that precious package? Of course he would! And if you've accepted the gift of Calvary, if you've determined that you want Jesus to be your Lord and Saviour—then He's going to come soon to claim you as the prize He paid so dearly for.

Someday very soon now, you and I are going to look up and see our King returning in the clouds. The great war will be over. Because of Calvary the universe will be safe again. Watching worlds will have acknowledged that Jesus Christ, born in the dusty land of Israel as a little human baby, nailed as a common criminal on a Roman cross, is now the victorious King of all God's universe.

And Jesus will take you home. The King will triumphantly return to heaven with His trophies, the fruits of His victory. Someplace beyond the stars is a mansion with the name "Finley" on it. And there's one for you as well. God and His Son promise it.

Read these lyrics to one of the most beautiful songs ever written about the return of our King; it's called *When He Comes Again*, and it's sung by a group named *Glad*:

And when He comes again,
He comes again to take us home.
And, oh, to know His love and grace,
To finally see His face—our King!
No longer through a dim and clouded glass,
When Jesus comes to take us home at last.

And when He comes again,
He comes again to take us home
In power and pure majesty,
All men will truly see He lives.
And every knee shall bow before the King,
And, oh, to praise His holy name we'll sing.

When He comes again,
When He comes again,

When He comes to claim His own,
When He comes to take us home.

When He comes all darkness fades away,
From the chains we are released.
And the glory of His holy name
Shall be so very clear to all who see.

When He comes again,
He comes again to take us home.
Sin and death no longer reign,
Heaven now is ours to gain again.
The weight of all our sins He gladly bore,
So Eden would be ours to share once more.

"When He Comes Again" written by John Keltonic (for my father) © 1991 JDK Music, Richmond, VA (ASCAP), reprinted by permission.

I could take fifty thousand more pages to talk with you about heaven, but space allows me to say only one thing about it. *Jesus* will be there. For a thousand years—and then right on into eternity—you and I will have the wonderful experience of discovering Jesus. He'll be a face-to-face Friend to you, the closest you've ever had.

Maybe there's something inside you that says, "Pastor Finley, I don't deserve it."

No, you don't. And neither do I. But on this hill called Calvary, Jesus created something called grace. Undeserved favor—that's what grace is.

A number of years ago a song became popular that talked about the home of Elvis Presley, "The King," as some music lovers called him. The name of the song was "Graceland." Today, as we quietly approach decision time together, let me suggest to you that really *heaven* should be called "Graceland." A home for you and for me, built on grace. A home made possible by the blood of Jesus, the real King. You and I could never deserve to be there, but for some wonderful reason, Jesus wants you. He wants me.

For a thousand years and beyond, we'll be reminded by the scars in the hands of Jesus that we're in Graceland. Because of the matchless love of Jesus, because of the great longing in His heart for you right now, you will be received with arms open wide.

Oh, friend, won't you say "Yes" right now? There's no better time to accept Jesus. To accept His gift. His grace. His promise of eternal life with Him. Say "Yes" now as we pray.

* * *

"Dear Lord, all through the pages of this adventure, we have thought of Jesus. We've made thrilling, life-changing discoveries about Him. But now the time has come to act upon what we've discovered.

"Father, You know every person reading these words. You know their need. Your Spirit has been gently tugging at their hearts. Please—just now—lead them into full surrender to You. Sweep away any barriers, any fears. Lead us each one into a new relationship with Jesus that will last and grow until that soon-promised day when Jesus our King returns to bring an end to the war that still rocks this planet.

"And Lord, thank You for heaven. We're eager to be there with You. We're so thankful that heaven—Graceland—is free to all. We accept that free gift right now and anticipate joyful fellowship with You and Jesus our King, because we accept Your gift in His precious name, Amen."